Dear Brian,

Thankyou for your inspiration through your photography.

Here is to your continued in all that you do!

Doug

★
GUERRILLA
SUCCESS

★ GUERRILLA SUCCESS

CelebrityPress®
Winter Park, Florida

CONTENTS

CHAPTER 20
TWELVE DIFFERENCES BETWEEN GUERRILLA WANNABE'S AND SUCCESSFUL GUERRILLA ENTREPRENEURS

INTRODUCTION

BY JEANNIE LEVINSON

THE HISTORY OF GUERRILLA MARKETING

"What is Guerrilla Marketing?" you may ask.

Guerrilla Marketing was a term first coined in 1984, by my late husband, Jay Conrad Levinson, who is now fondly referred to as "The Father of Guerrilla Marketing", but who exactly was Jay Conrad Levinson....

For those who were fans of the hit TV Series *"Mad Men"*, many think of him as the "Donald Draper" of Chicago.

In the 1960's, Jay served as the Vice President, and Creative Director of two of the biggest advertising agencies in the world; first, Leo Burnett Advertising, (both in Chicago and then opening their European office in London), and later, J. Walter Thompson Advertising back in Chicago.

During his time there, he led the teams responsible for working on and creating some of the most Iconic advertising of that era; including: The Marlboro Man (considered the best marketing campaign ever created), Sears Die Hard Battery, The Good Hands of Allstate, The Friendly Skies of United, Tony the Tiger, The Pillsbury Doughboy, Mr. Clean, Snap Crackle & Pop, The Jolly Green Giant, Charlie the Tuna, Morris the Cat, and many other critters still beloved to this day.

Jay was born in Detroit on Feb 10, 1933, but his family moved to the South Side of Chicago when he was just a baby. There, despite his Dad being a "Cubbie," Jay grew up a devout "White Sox" fan and became a Pitcher in the Minor Leagues.

After receiving degrees in both Psychology and Law, he came to the conclusion that he didn't want to pursue a career in Law, and eventually developed his personal philosophy that "Every day spent in Court, was subtracted from your days spent in Heaven."

Jay first discovered his love for writing when he served in the Military in the Counter Intelligence Corp. Part of his duties, after spying on subversive groups, included writing up derogatory reports of his findings. He admitted that although he loved the James Bond type of 'cloak and dagger' excitement it entailed. His real passion came through when it was time to write up the reports.

After his discharge from the Army, he sought work as a copywriter, and eventually found himself working with Hugh Hefner. He launched the *"Playboy"* campaign "What Sort of Man Reads Playboy" to help elevate its perception from seedy to GQ. For helping to open the first Playboy Mansion in Chicago, "Hef" offered him a choice between a $1,000 bonus or Mansion Key Number # 1, to which Jay astutely responded, "I'll take both." Jay also worked on launching *Rolling Stone Magazine*.

One winter day, while sitting at a Bus Stop in downtown Chicago, with ice forming on his nose, he noted that the temperature had not been above freezing for that entire month. He suddenly had an epiphany. He didn't have to stay in Chicago, realizing that he could write copy from anywhere in the country including places where it never snowed.

So in 1971, he packed up his family and moved to the San Francisco Bay Area. He was familiar with its balmy weather from being stationed at the Presidio when he was in the Military in the 50's. During that time, he discovered that by working from his home, he could make more money and accomplish in three days at his home office, what used to take him five days at his corporate office. This was because, at home, he was spared having to read memos, attend meetings, or be disrupted by sweet people coming into his office just to shoot the breeze.

One of the things he took the greatest pride in, was that for the next 40 years, he never again worked more than a three-day week. This freed him up to follow two of his other favorite passions, which was whitewater rafting in the summer, and skiing in the winter. To him, obtaining this work /life balance, was the epitome of "Success."

He felt there was nothing special about him, and that anyone could do what he was doing, so he wrote a book about it called: *" Secrets of Successful Freelancing."*

When the U.S. Recession of the early 1970's came about, Jay, responding to the need of so many who found themselves out of work, and wrote the book *"Earning Money Without a Job."* This led to him being asked to teach a college course called *"Alternatives to the 9 to 5 Job."*

After retiring from the Advertising Industry, Jay ended up for the next ten years as a fulltime professor teaching Marketing at the University of California extension division in Berkley.

One day, when he came to class, a group of his students came up to him and said, "Mr. Levinson, can you recommend a marketing book for us? One thing we all have in common, we are all long-haired hippies, but we have brilliant ideas. However, we also have empty pockets. All of the books we have seen are for huge Fortune 500 companies that have three hundred thousand dollars a month or more to invest in their marketing, and that certainly is not us. Can you recommend a book to help us?"

Jay promised his students that he would find a book for them. Since there was no such thing as Google or Amazon in the 1980's, Jay spent the next several days scouring the local book stores and libraries, but much to his dismay, was unable to find a single book written for small businesses or young startups. But Jay had made a promise to his students, so he decided he would write a book just for them.

He wrote down all the ways he had learned to market products, and came up with a list of "437 ways to use unconventional low cost or no-cost marketing strategies." He thought to himself, this was a lot of great content, but a terrible title for a book. So he decided to call it *"Guerrilla Marketing"* because, just like guerrillas in warfare, who had to fight the larger government-sponsored military using limited resources, so these students had to go up against the larger corporations with limited budgets.

Soon the concept of "Guerrilla Marketing" took on a life of its own. What was initially written strictly for the hippie kids in his class became a world-wide phenomenon, selling over 22 million copies in 64 languages. Named one of the top ten most important business books ever written, it is now required reading in most MBA programs worldwide. Together, Jay and I have gone on to author or co-author over 125 books, and the "Guerrilla" series is considered one of the most successful business book series in history.

By the way, those hippie kids with the brilliant ideas eventually grew up, and built successful businesses of their own... some of their names?.... Bill Gates of Microsoft, Larry Ellison of Oracle and Steve Jobs of Apple... just to name a few. Now you can learn the very same concepts from the man that taught Steve Jobs how to: *"Think Different."*

So, what exactly is "Guerrilla Marketing"? ...

- **Guerrilla Marketing** is going after conventional goals, using unconventional means.

- **Guerrilla Marketing** is low cost or no-cost tactics and strategies.
- **Guerrilla Marketing** is stealth, surprising, unexpected and viral.
- **Guerrilla Marketing** is the truth made fascinating.
- **Guerrilla Marketing** is the art of getting people to change their minds.
- **Guerrilla Marketing** is a process not an event.
- **Guerrilla Marketing** has a beginning, but if you do it right, has no end.
- **Guerrilla Marketing** is a circle that starts with your great idea for a business and then continues with the blessed patronage of repeat and referral business. If your marketing is not a circle it will become a straight line that can lead straight to the bankruptcy courts.
- **Guerrilla marketing** is out-of-the-box thinking, using time, energy, imagination and information instead of a huge budget.

An example of a true Guerrilla who leaned on his fertile imagination to market his business, is the story of a man who had a furniture store.

One day he came to work, and noticed a huge building being erected on the right side of his store. Later, to his dismay, he learned that this building was also a furniture store, much larger than his. Shortly after that, another building started going up, and it too was another furniture store.

If that wasn't bad enough, one day he arrived to work and noticed that the store on his right hand unfurled a banner that read, "Monster clearance sale prices marked down 50%." "Oh my, 50%! How can I compete with that?" he questioned, but then he turned to his left and saw the other store had also unfurled a banner that read " Grand Opening Prices as slashed 75%." "Wow!" he exclaimed, "Their banner is bigger than my entire store!" But he was a Guerrilla, so instead of getting discouraged or depressed, he started thinking. Using his imagination, he went back into his store and created his own banner and hung it out in front of his store and it read.... MAIN ENTRANCE.

Instead of using any money, this creative guerrilla used the brute force of a powerful imagination to beat his competition... Now that's Guerrilla Marketing!

When Jay wrote the very first *Guerrilla Marketing* book and started speaking around the world, he never dreamed the global impact it would eventually have, but he soon discovered how in a very startling way.

While on an Eastern European speaking tour, we were traveling to Romania to give a talk. When we stepped off the plane and into the Limo waiting on the tarmac, we were suddenly surrounded by police and military vehicles. Jay started to panic, thinking that perhaps it was some kind of military coup. The host turned to him and said "Why no Mr. Levinson, they are all here for you." "Uh, oh" Jay thought, "What in the world have I done wrong?" thinking he was about to be arrested.

"Why are they here for me?" questioned Jay. "Don't you know?" replied the host. "No why?" Jay responded. "Well this is a police escort, Mr. Levinson, because you are considered a National Hero in our country," the host explained. "Really, me? But why is that?" asked Jay incredulously.

When the Limo turned down one of the main streets in Bucharest, we were greeted by huge billboards, with Jay's picture on them saying "JAY CONRAD LEVINSON COMES TO ROMANIA" and people lining both sides of the street waving white handkerchiefs as we drove by. "I don't understand what any of this is all about." Jay exclaimed.

As it turns out, after Jay wrote *"Guerrilla Marketing"* in 1984, he started doing lectures about it in the San Francisco Bay area. One day, a little Romanian woman came up to him after the lecture, asking for his autograph and requesting permission to translate his book into the Romanian language. " Of course you can." Jay said, never giving it another thought.

Apparently, after this little lady translated the book, she smuggled it into then Communist-ruled Romania. It was then reprinted underground and distributed secretly among the common people. These people had been under Communist rule since the '60's and an entire generation had only worked for "The State" and they had no idea how to start and run a business of their own.

They used Jay's book, *"Guerrilla Marketing"* as one of the ways to gain the knowledge, and then the confidence that they needed to start the "Romanian Revolution of 1989" to come out from behind the Iron Curtain, break free from Communism, become Entrepreneurs, and rebuild their economy.

Jay had no clue! Here he was, a little old man, who sat at his desk at his home office typing away on his manual typewriter, never knowing that the words he was typing would one day affect the politics of an entire country half way across the planet!

So all of us should carefully consider this, we may never know the impact of what we say or do, will one day have on others without us ever even realizing it.

The "Guerrilla" brand is now related to much more than just "marketing," and now refers to doing almost anything in an "unconventional" way.

I have always been a "behind the scenes" kind of person, but when Jay was diagnosed with terminal cancer in 2010, he took me in his arms and whispered to me, "Jeannie, You have always been the wind beneath my wings, but now, you need to become the bird, so that you can fly for me."

After a valiant 2-1/2 year battle, Jay, at age 80, passed away in my arms on October 10, 2013. It has now become my passion to keep Jay's legacy alive, I promised him I would not let his "Guerrilla" brand die with him.

Part of that legacy is the book you are now holding in your hand. The first volume of this collaborative book with Celebrity Branding, *Guerrilla Success,* is a compilation written by a variety of Guerrilla Entrepreneurs, who have used unconventional wisdom to find success in their lives, and now, they are passing that guerrilla wisdom on to you.

Jay was a very humble man... but he left a huge footprint on this earth. Now it's your turn.

Here's to YOUR *Guerrilla Success!*

Jeannie

Jeannie Levinson, Co-Founder; CEO
Guerrilla Marketing International

CHAPTER 1

WHAT ARE GUERRILLA ENTREPRENEURS?

BY JAY CONRAD LEVINSON AND
JEANNIE LEVINSON

THE GUERRILLA ENTREPRENEUR

The guerrilla entrepreneur has left behind many things he's grown to love – or hate. He's embraced new ways of thinking, new ways of working, new ways of living. He well knows that he's left behind an age characterized by a worship of profits, a surfeit of working hours, and a neglect of family and self. Before we go on, we want you to know that in this chapter, because so many entrepreneurs are women and because of their impressive success rate, the word "he" refers equally to male and female genders.

Sure, the guerrilla entrepreneur still aims towards profits, but not at the expense of draconian working hours or the sacrificing of precious living time. He defines success not only by the standard notion of finances, but also the blessed notion of balance – between work and leisure, work and family, work and humanity, work and self. He seeks and finds success beyond the profit-and-loss statement, beyond the workplace.

Today, there are more entrepreneurs than ever, but few true guerrilla entrepreneurs. The option to be either probably did not exist for your parents or your grandparents, because the path to it had not been blazed by technology and social enlightenment. The Puritan work ethic of your ancestors has gone by the wayside along with the Puritans. That work ethic had no place for balance, only for hard work. The guerrilla entrepreneur's work ethic includes both. His hallmarks are the best of the old ways, such as sane working hours, time for his family, and humane treatment of employees – with the best of the new ways, such as time-saving technologies, advanced and mobile communication techniques, and enlightened attitudes toward work and social life.

Guerrilla entrepreneurs who cuddle up to the new easy-to-afford, easy-to-use technologies discover opportunities as plentiful and sparkling as raindrops in spring. They have learned that aiming high isn't as important as aiming sensibly. This allows many of them to reach their goals sooner than they expected.

They make profits the third priority, well ahead of sales and leads, but well behind humanity and balance. Their enterprises are flexible, innovative, unconventional, up-to-the-second in technology, low in overhead costs, dependent, interactive, generous, enjoyable and money making. One of their objectives is to stay that way.

Look at the entrepreneurs around you. If you can't see many, it's because they are not guerrillas; instead they're buried in work, rarely coming up for the fresh air of free time. Guerrilla entrepreneurs seem to be happier with their work and appear to care like crazy about satisfying the needs of their customers. They stay in touch constantly with their customers. They express their passion for working with excellence and transform it into profits. Their long-term goals are lofty. Those goals exist in the future. Their short-term goals are even loftier. Those goals exist in the present – for that is the domain of guerrilla entrepreneurs. That is where their goals are to be found in abundance.

They thrive on the non-traditional, do the unconventional if the conventional is nonsensical, and know that the real name of the game is the journey – the best of all goals. When the journey is the goal, you can begin with work that satisfies you, spend time enjoying activities other than that work you love, and gain a remarkable freedom from work-related stress. You'll be able to maintain good health and not participate in recessions.

The goals of the guerrilla entrepreneur:
- work that is satisfying
- enough money to enjoy freedom from worry about it
- health good enough to take for granted
- a bonding with others where you give and receive love and support
- fun that is not pursued but is in the essence of daily living
- longevity to appreciate with wisdom that which you have achieved

TO BE A GUERRILLA ENTREPRENEUR: YOU'VE GOT TO KNOW WHAT ONE REALLY IS

Guerrilla entrepreneurs knows that the journey is the goal.

They also realize that they are in control of their enterprise, not the other way around, and that if they are dissatisfied with their journey, they are missing the point of the journey itself. Unlike old-fashioned enterprises, which often required gigantic sacrifices for the sake of the goal, guerrilla enterprises place the goal of a pleasant journey ahead of the mere notion of sacrifices.

Guerrilla entrepreneurs achieve balance from the very start.

They build free time into their work schedule so that balance is part of their enterprise. They respect their leisure time as much as their work time, never allowing too much of one to interfere with the other. Traditional entrepreneurs always placed work ahead of leisure and showed no respect for their own personal freedom. Guerrillas cherish their freedom as much as their work.

Guerrilla entrepreneurs are not in a hurry.

A false need for speed frequently undermines even the best-conceived strategies. Haste makes waste and sacrifices quality. Guerrillas are fully aware that patience is their ally, and they have planned intelligently to eliminate most emergencies that call for moving fast. Their pace is always steady but never rushed.

Guerrilla entrepreneurs use stress as a benchmark.

If they feel any stress, they know they must be going about things in the wrong way. Guerrilla entrepreneurs do not accept stress as part of doing business and recognize any stress as a warning sign that something's the matter -- in the work plan of the guerrilla or in the business itself. Adjustments are made to eliminate the cause of the stress rather than the stress itself.

Guerrilla entrepreneurs look forward to work.

They have a love affair with their work and consider themselves blessed to be paid for doing the work they do. They are good at their work, energizing their passion for it in a quest to learn more about it and improve their understanding of it, thereby increasing their skills. The guerrilla entrepreneur doesn't think about retirement, for never would they want to stop doing work they love.

Guerrilla entrepreneurs have no weaknesses.

They are effective in every aspect of their enterprise because they have filled in the gaps between their strengths and talents with people who abound in the prowess they lack. They are very much the team player and team up with guerrillas like themselves who share the team spirit and possess complementary skills. They value their teammates as much as old-fashioned entrepreneurs valued their independence.

Guerrilla entrepreneurs are fusion-oriented.

They are always on the alert to fuse their business with other enterprises in town, in America, in the world. They are willing to combine marketing efforts, production skills, information, leads, mailing lists and anything else to increase their effectiveness and marketing reach while reducing the cost of achieving those goals. Their fusion efforts are intentionally short-term and rarely permanent. In their business relationships, instead of thinking marriage, they think "fling."

Guerrilla entrepreneurs don't kid themselves.

They know that if they overestimate their own abilities, they run the risk of skimping on the quality they represent to their customers, employees, investors, suppliers and fusion partners. They force themselves to face reality on a daily basis and realize that all of their business practices must always be evaluated in the glaring light of what is really happening, instead of what should be happening.

Guerrilla entrepreneurs live in the present.

They are well-aware of the past, very enticed by the future, but the here and now is where they reside, embracing the technologies of the present, leaving future technologies on the horizon right where they belong -- on the horizon until later, when they are ripe and ready. They are alert to the new, wary of the avant-garde, and only wooed from the old by improvement, not merely change.

Guerrilla entrepreneurs understand the precious nature of time.

They don't buy into the old lie that time is money and know in their heart that time is far more important than money. They know that instead, time is life. They are aware that their customers and prospects feel the same way about time, so they respect theirs and wouldn't dare waste it. As a practicing guerrilla, they are the epitome of efficiency but never let it interfere with their effectiveness.

Guerrilla entrepreneurs always operate according to a plan.

They know who they are, where they are going, and how they will get there. They are prepared, know that anything can and will happen, and can deal with the barriers to entrepreneurial success because their plan has foreseen them and shown exactly how to surmount them. Guerrillas reevaluate their plan regularly and don't hesitate to make changes in it, though commitment to the plan is part of their very being.

Guerrilla entrepreneurs are flexible.

They are guided by a strategy for success, and know the difference between a guide and a master. When it is necessary for change, the guerrilla changes, accepting change as part of the status quo, not ignoring or battling it. They are able to adapt to new situations, realize that service is whatever their customers want it to be, and know that inflexible things become brittle and break.

Guerrilla entrepreneurs aim for results more than growth.

They are focused upon profitability and balance, vitality and improvement, value and quality more than size and growth. Their plan calls for steadily increasing profits without a sacrifice of personal time, so their actions are oriented to hitting those targets instead of growing for the sake of growth alone. They are wary of becoming large and don't equate hugeness with excellence.

Guerrilla entrepreneurs are dependent upon many people.

They know that the age of the lone wolf entrepreneur, independent and proud of it, has passed. Guerrillas are very dependent upon their fusion business partners, their employees, their customers, their suppliers, and their mentors. They got where they are with their own wings, their own determination, their own smarts, and, as guerrillas, with a little help from a lot of friends.

Guerrilla entrepreneurs are constantly learning.

A seagull flies in circles in the sky, looking for food in an endless quest. When it finally finds food, the seagull lands, then eats its fill. When it has completed the meal, the seagull returns to the sky, only to fly in circles again, searching for food although it has eaten. Humans have only one instinct that compares: the need for constant learning. Guerrilla entrepreneurs have this need in spades.

Guerrilla entrepreneurs are passionate about work.

They have an enthusiasm for what they do that is apparent to everyone who sees their work. This enthusiasm spreads to everyone who works with them, even to their customers. In its purest form, this enthusiasm is best expressed as the word passion -- an intense feeling that burns within them and is manifested in the devotion they demonstrate towards their business.

Guerrilla entrepreneurs are focused on the goal.

They know that balance does not come easily, and that they must rid themselves of the values and expectations of their ancestors. To do this, they must remain focused upon their journey, seeing the future clearly, at the same time concentrating upon the present. They are aware that the minutiae of life and business can distract them, so they do what is necessary to make those distractions only momentary.

Guerrilla entrepreneurs are disciplined about the tasks at hand.

They are keenly aware that every time they write a task on their daily calendar, it is a promise they are making to themselves. As guerrillas who don't kid themselves, they keep those promises, knowing that the achievement of their goals will be more than an adequate reward for their discipline. They find it easy to be disciplined because of the payback offered by the leisure that follows.

Guerrilla entrepreneurs are well-organized at home and at work.

They don't waste valuable time looking for items that have been misplaced, so they organize as they work and as new work comes to them. Their sense of organization is fueled by the efficiency that results from it. While they are always organized, the guerrilla never squanders precious time by over-organizing.

Guerrilla entrepreneurs have an upbeat attitude.

Because they know that life is unfair, problems arise, to err is human, and the cool shall inherit the Earth, they manage to take obstacles in stride, keeping their perspective and their sense of humor. Their ever-present optimism is grounded in an ability to perceive the positive side of things, recognizing the negative, but never dwelling there. Their positivity is contagious.

THE WAY OF THE GUERRILLA

To reiterate, the goals of 21st century guerrilla entrepreneurs are work that is satisfying, enough money to enjoy freedom from worry about it, health good enough to take for granted, a bonding with others where you give and receive love and support, fun that is not pursued but is the essence of daily living and longevity to appreciate with wisdom that which you have achieved.

THAT IS ESSENCE OF GUERRILLA SUCCESS!

About Jay

Jay Conrad Levinson was the author of the best-selling marketing series in history, *"Guerrilla Marketing,"* plus 125 other business books. His books have sold more than 22 million copies worldwide. And his guerrilla concepts have influenced marketing so much that his books appear in 64 languages and are required reading in MBA programs worldwide.

Jay taught guerrilla marketing for ten years at the extension division of the University of California in Berkeley. He was a practitioner of it in the United States — as Senior VP at J. Walter Thompson, and in Europe, as Creative Director of Leo Burnett Advertising.

A winner of first prizes in all the media, he was a part of the creative teams that made household names of many of the most famous brands in history: The Marlboro Man, The Pillsbury Doughboy, Mr. Clean, Tony the Tiger, Allstate's good hands, United's friendly skies, the Sears Diehard battery, Morris the Cat, and the Jolly Green Giant – just to name a few.

He was the Chairman and Co-Founder with his wife, Jeannie, of Guerrilla Marketing International, which includes their Website, (www.gmarketing.com) and a series of Books, CDs, DVD's, Webinars, Bootcamps, Facebook:Group (Guerrilla Marketing Official Group), The Annual Guerrilla Global Summit, The Annual Guerrilla Marketing Cruise, The Guerrilla Marketing Business University and The Guerrilla Marketing Association — a marketing support system for small business consisting of local chapter mastermind meetings located across the country.

Most of all, Guerrilla Marketing is a way for business owners to spend less, get more, and achieve substantial profits.

The best guerrilla to transform you into a guerrilla marketer is – "The Father of Guerrilla Marketing": Jay Conrad Levinson!

About Jeannie

Jeannie Levinson, is the Co-Founder and CEO of "Guerrilla Marketing International, "The Guerrilla Marketing Association" and "The Guerrilla Marketing Business University."

She is the Co-Author with her late husband, Jay Conrad Levinson, of the updated classic book *Guerrilla Marketing* which is required reading in many MBA programs worldwide, with over 22 million copies sold in 64 languages.

Guerrilla Marketing was recently named by *Inc. Magazine* as one of the top ten most influential business books of all time.

She has also authored other bestselling books including: *Guerrilla Marketing for Free; Guerrilla Creativity / Marketing with Memes; The Start Up Guide to Guerrilla Marketing; The Guerrilla Marketing Field Guide* and *Guerrilla Marketing Remix / The Best of Guerrilla Marketing.*

She is a Licensed GM Master Trainer, Certified GM Coach, Public Speaker, Workshop Leader and a successful Entrepreneur for over 40 years.

She and her husband, Jay, have traveled to over 67 countries teaching the low cost/no cost, unconventional principles of Guerrilla Marketing around the world.

CONTACT INFO:

- Guerrilla Marketing International
- jeannie@gmarketing.com
- www.gmarketing.com
- www.guerrillaglobalsummit.com
- Facebook: Guerrilla Marketing Official Group

CHAPTER 2

THE PITFALLS OF BEING AN ENTREPRENEUR

BY JAY CONRAD LEVINSON AND JEANNIE LEVINSON

Pitfall #1: The Time Trap

As much as people revere leisure time, they have less of it than ever, averaging much less leisure time than they had in the past. Here we are jumping up and glorifying the three-day week when increasing numbers of Americans are wondering how to get out from under the six-day week. Habits are much easier to form than they are to break. "I'll just work 60 hours a week for now, and then I'll cut back later." . . . Won't happen.

Pitfall #2: The Large Lure

You'll be offered chances to earn more money, expand, take on more people, move to a larger space and transform from an entrepreneurial endeavor to a large, corporate-type entity. Hey, it's your life, but you've got to turn in your guerrilla credentials if you opt for large rather than free, for bigness over balance.

Pitfall #3: The Money Morass

Money alters human behavior to the point that it causes well-meaning owners of small business, bound for success, to veer in the direction of financial success, steamrollering any chances of emotional, marital, parental or social success. Money, being easier to attain than balance, is more frequently sought. Those in pursuit of it find that the prices they pay are worth far more than money. Of all the pitfalls, The Money Morass is the deepest, darkest and biggest.

Pitfall #4: The Burnout Barrier

You'll search your soul to come up with a method for providing your livelihood and you'll set up shop with all the right intentions. You'll work hard and smart and your rewards will be fruitful. But somewhere along the way, you will have lost some of your initial enthusiasm for your work. You'll continue on because you've been successful, but you'll bring less and less joy to your work. The thrill is gone. There is no more enthusiasm. You burned out. What to do now is something else. If the spark is gone, get yourself another dream. Enthusiasm will fuel your fires, and if it is absent, the fire in your soul will go out—the fire that was the key to your success. Guerrillas know that they can relight the fire for a new venture, and that studies prove that the more you love what you do, the better you'll do it. So if you no longer feel the love, end the relationship and start another.

Pitfall #5: The Humanity Hindrance

We hope like crazy that you never lose your personal warmth, your sense of humor, or your love of other human beings in your quest to become a successful entrepreneur. Sadly, the world has more than enough tales of individuals who left a trail of shattered people on their climb to the top. The guerrilla's priority list places people ahead of business, family ahead of business, love ahead of business, self ahead of business. Keeping your eyes on the bottom line should not make them beady. Putting your heart in your work should not turn it to stone. Attaining everything on your wish list should not put you upon anybody's enemy list. An executive we knew at a Fortune 500 company had a glass eye.

When we asked which was the glass eye, we were told, "It's the warm one." There is no rule that says you give up your humanity as the dues for achieving entrepreneurial success.

Pitfall #6: The Focus Foil

It is not difficult to lose your focus, to set it upon a false goal, a tangential journey leading away from your dreams. You become so involved in the details of your operation that you deviate from your prime thrust. Your time becomes gobbled up by details instead of broad strokes. The idea is to grow your mind as you grow your business, but maintain your direction.

Pitfall #7: The Perfection Pit

High atop our own list of time-wasters, life-stealers, and company-ruiners are perfectionists and those in the pursuit of perfection. We are all for excellence and admire perfection in a bowling game or classroom attendance – two areas where perfection is possible. Guerrillas try to be perfect, but don't spend all their time and energy attaining it. They know that the world is teeming with entrepreneurs who spend half their time polishing the unpolishable, steeped in the unnecessary, devoted to the unattainable. May your enterprise be free from imperfections and perfectionists.

Pitfall #8: The Selling Snare

The selling snare is a trap that forces you to sell the same thing over and over again. The guerrilla's way around it: make multiple sales with one effort. Instead of selling a single issue of a magazine, sell a subscription. Guerrillas do all in their power to develop products or services that must be purchased on a regular basis. Many offerings are sold with the repeat sales built right in, from our Guerrilla Marketing Newsletter to cable television, from cleaning services to diaper service, from insurance coverage to gardening, from swimming pool maintenance to dental care.

The idea is to apply the ultimate in selling skills so that your one-time sale can lead to years and years of profits. If you fall into the trap of selling single shots only, you'll be spending more time selling than enjoying the benefits of your efforts.

Pitfall #9: The Leisure Lure

Don't kid yourself into believing that leisure time is automatically a good thing. Leisure time, when you don't know what do to with it, can lead to a wide variety of problems – from boredom to substance abuse. Truth be told, many people actually enjoy their work time more than their leisure time because at least they know what they'll be doing with their work time, but haven't a clue as to how to spend their leisure hours. Guerrillas do have a clue. And a hobby. And a slew of interests beyond working and earning money. They enjoy their leisure almost as much as their work, because they are working at something they love and because they've given a lot of thought to what they'll do with their free time. They know that free time by itself can be a drag.

Pitfall #10 The Retirement Ruse

Horrid but true: more than 75 percent of retirees die within two years of their retirement. When they retire from work, it's as though they also retire from life. Don't make the mistake of planning for retirement. Plan on cutting down, on easing off, but not on quitting altogether. Working keeps you sharp, keeps your brain in shape. Ceasing to work allows your brain to atrophy. What are most retirees concerned with? Well, 38 percent say they don't have enough money. Another 29 percent say they're fearful of not staying healthy. Eight percent say they have too much time on their hands and they're bored. And eight percent figure they probably won't live long enough to enjoy life. Guerrillas have enough money because they put retirement into the same category as imprisonment. The money continues to flow into their lives long after their cohorts have retired. They stay healthy because continuing to hone the edge caused by work results in the maintenance of health and increased longevity. They do not suffer from the problem of too much time, having just enough for work, just enough for play. And they have been enjoying life all along because they've been engaged in the work they love, a trademark of the guerrilla entrepreneur. In nature, nothing ever retires, and as we are getting closer to understanding our own relationship with nature, we are understanding that retirement is unhealthy and contraindicated in anyone with brain waves. As an entrepreneur, you are your own boss. No one is going to make you retire. What happens if you are simply no longer interested in the business? Retire from it – then move on to another dream. Just don't retire from life itself. The trap of planning for retirement is like planning your own slow suicide – brought upon by inactivity.

TEN DIRTY LIES YOU HAVE KNOWN AND LOVED

1. TIME IS MONEY.
2. OWNING A BUSINESS MEANS WORKAHOLISM.
3. MARKETING IS EXPENSIVE.
4. BIG CORPORATIONS ARE LIKE WOMBS.
5. YOUTH IS BETTER THAN AGE.
6. YOU NEED A JOB.
7. HEAVEN IS IN THE AFTERLIFE.
8. THE PURPOSE OF EDUCATION IS TO TEACH FACTS.
9. IF YOU WANT IT DONE RIGHT, DO IT YOURSELF.
10. RETIREMENT IS A GOOD THING.

[Note: For biographical details on the authors, please refer to p.30.]

CHAPTER 3

GUERRILLA SUCCESS IN THE NEW MILLENNIUM

BY JAY CONRAD LEVINSON AND JEANNIE LEVINSON

Two things of which you can be very certain in this new millennium is that… business will be a lot harder, and that… business will be a lot easier.

It will be *harder* because of FIVE factors:

1. TIME
Time will become magnified in importance. The luxury of spare time at work is a luxury of the past. Spare time will be revered, but not at work. You will be unable to help but notice the new awareness of time by almost everyone. Customers will demand and expect speed. You will, too.

2. CONTACT
Less face-to-face contact will remove much of the warmth of working. People now get over half their messages by non-verbal communication. This means that non-verbal communications will be less accurate; verbal accuracy more valuable. The joy of social interaction will be much abated.

3. CHANGE
Change will be thrust upon us and much that we counted on

before will no longer hold forth. Even things we learn will only be true for a short time before surpassed by new truths. The genius will not be in learning something but in learning one thing after another. If you can't adapt, you aren't cut out to be a guerrilla.

4. TALENT
Talent will be diffused as top people will trade the vitality of a huge corporation for the tranquility of working at home. Well and good for them, but for guerrilla entrepreneurs, this means all the big brains won't be under one roof. You'll have to scout them out.

5. TECHNOLOGY
Technology will be more important in your life and you'll have to understand it to take full advantage of it. But technical things are becoming easier to use, user manuals are written more clearly, and the nature of training (repetition will be your friend for life) has improved. If you're technophobic, see a technoshrink.

The FIVE ways that business will be *easier* are really five thousand ways, but for purposes of time, let's just go with five right here:

1. TIME
You will have more time to do what really must be done rather than busywork – because technical advancements will allow for it. Your network of independent contractors will also free up more of your time. Use it to increase your profits, make your business better, or just plain enjoy yourself.

2. VALUES
Values will change and they will be more in keeping with your own guerrilla values. In the 20th century, the main value was placed on making money. In the 21st century, that priority takes a back seat to the human values of happiness at work, free time, family, spirituality. As you are discovering, profit-seeking will

never be eliminated, only reprioritized.

3. ADVANCEMENTS
New advancements in business, both psychological and technological, will make the workplace more exciting and easier to use, even enjoyable. Flex-time, webinars, tele-conferencing, digital marketing and social media, will make for less crowded commuting if you commute at all. The virtual office is the at-home office. And it's here now.

4. PROCEDURES
Streamlined procedures will keep your work life efficient, organized, simple and fast. You won't waste time or effort at work because you'll have learned to become an efficient working machine, and as a guerrilla entrepreneur, you'll realize that the whole purpose of streamlining is to add effectiveness.

5. PEOPLE
You will deal with smarter people and they'll be fewer in number. Your workplace won't be populated with paper-shufflers. Your at-home business will put you into contact with bright, talented entrepreneurs who made the break from the corporate life and are doing very well, just like you.

THE WAY OF THE GUERRILLA GIVES YOU AN EDGE

You've got the guerrilla's edge in insight.

You've given thought to your priorities. You aren't going to be misled by the entrepreneurial myths involving overwork, overgrowth and overextending your reach. You realize that your journey is your destination and that your plan is your roadmap. This insight will help you maintain your passion.

You've got the guerrilla's edge in relationships.

Every sale you make leads to a lasting relationship. Every customer you get is going to be a customer for life. Your sales and even your profits will probably go up and down, but your number of relationships will constantly go up, and your sales and profits will eventually follow.

You've got the guerrilla's edge in service.

You see your service from your customer's point of view, not merely from your own. You realize that your service gives you an enormous competitive advantage over those who may be larger, but less devoted to making and keeping customers delighted with your company. You know well the power of word-of-mouth marketing and how it equates with excellent service.

You've got the guerrilla's edge in flexibility.

You are not enslaved by company policies and by precedent. Instead, you are fast on your feet, sensitive to customer needs, aware of flexibility as a tool for building relationships, profits and your overall company. You are guided by the situation at hand and not by the way things were done in the past. Your flexibility adds to the passion that others feel about your company.

You've got the guerrilla's edge in follow-up.

You don't have to be reminded about the number of potential relationships that are destroyed by customers being ignored after they made a purchase. Rather than ignoring them, you pay attention to them, remind them of how glad you are that they're customers, and pepper them with special offers, inside information and care. They never feel ignored by you and reciprocate by never ignoring your company when it comes to repeat purchases or referrals.

You have the guerrilla's edge in cooperation.

You see other businesses as potential partners of yours, as firms that can help you as you help them. You don't keep your eye peeled for competitors to annihilate but for businesses to team up with and form networks. Your attitude will help you prosper in an era when people are forming small businesses in droves.

You have the guerrilla's edge in patience.

As a guerrilla, you are not in a hurry, never in a rush. You know how important time is, but you also know how speed usually results in diminished quality. Because of your planning, you are able to avoid emergencies and high pressure situations. Patience is one of your staunchest allies as a guerrilla.

You have the guerrilla's edge in economy.

You know how to market without investing a bundle of hard-earned money. You have learned the value of time and energy as substitutes for large budgets. You realize that in most business activity, you have a choice of any two of these three factors: speed, economy and quality. You always opt for economy and quality. Your patience helps you economize.

You have the guerrilla's edge in timeliness.

You run a streamlined operation, devoid of fluff or unnecessary work. Your comfort with technology allows you to operate at maximum effectiveness. Your business is a state-of-the-art enterprise because it operates in the environment of today rather than ten years ago. Although you maintain your focus upon your plan, you know the magic of proper timing and are able to make adjustments so that you are there just when customers need you.

You have the guerrilla's edge in commitment.

This commitment will set you apart from many other businesses. It will help you achieve your aims with certainty. It is so powerful that you feel passion towards the commitment itself – enabling the passion to power your commitment, and the commitment to power your passion. Without this inner commitment, even the best plans may go awry. With it, plans turn into a bright reality.

The closer you examine it, the more you see that the way of the guerrilla is a way illuminated by the radiant light of love – love of self, work, family, others, freedom, independence, life. The guerrilla has a lifelong love affair with life. The deeper and more heartfelt his love, the more he is capable of generating the fiery and exquisite passion that fuels his fires.

LOVE IS THE KEY

1. **Love of self**
2. **Love of work**
3. **Love of family**
4. **Love of play**
5. **Love of freedom**
6. **Love of independence**
7. **Love of friends**
8. **Love of customers and employees**
9. **Love of a higher power**
10. **Love of life**

THE GUERRILLA ENTREPRENEUR'S LIFE IS A LOVE STORY, FOR LOVE ILLUMINATES THE WAY OF THE GUERRILLA.

[Note: For biographical details on the authors, please refer to p.30.]

CHAPTER 4

HOW TO DEVELOP A STRONG GUERRILLA SUCCESS CONCEPT?
– SEVEN STEPS TO FOLLOW, FIVE BEHAVIORS TO ADOPT

BY IGOR NIKOLOSKI

We are living in a world that is extremely complicated and highly competitive. Technology is developing so fast that it is too hard to follow even by reading, not to mention implementing all the technology innovation in larger systems. The world economy and macro-economic trends were not pleasant in the past few years and they don't seem to be improving much in the near future. But is it important to you? People are trying to do their best, but they are being lost in their efforts. And still, there are some people and companies that can generate a strong growth rate in this complicated environment while others can't. Some grow in negative macroeconomic trends, while some fall even in the positive macroeconomic trends. Some concepts work well in crisis as well as in good times, and have some universal value that is long lasting, while some look "lost in space" without clear direction, and exhibit chaotic behavior.

There is a lot of innovation in the world but there is limited integration and implementation. It is all about systems, their relations and cause-effect sequences.

It's all about understanding and integrating in the desired direction. It's all about your mission.

In the past 15 years, I have developed several brands and companies using the same universal principles and behaviors, and they resulted in double-digit growth rates many years in a row, no matter the negative or positive economic environment. New companies, new ideas, new brands and businesses are too small to feel the global climate. There will always be good potential on the market for the right brands, companies, people, products, services...concepts. Customers like concepts. From here, I would like to share with you secrets of my GUERRILLA SUCCESS based on mission-driven concept development.

*** *** ***

I remember 5 years ago, my parents decided to retire and the management of the company was left to me and my younger brother. I was responsible for the strategic marketing operations and general management. It was very logical as at that time I had 10 years of experience in several companies and industries – as CEO, Marketing Manager and Marketing Assistant – and before I had graduated in International Marketing with the best graduation thesis among the multi-national class at the university in the Netherlands.

All the previous years before I took over the management of my family business, I learned, read and worked with a strong imagination about how to build our family restaurant business and make it a strong national brand. I spent more than 15 years in reading, thinking, using my imagination, studying and learning in this direction. Finally, it happened. I was very happy on the first day and on the next I had to make the first big decision – to define the course and the strategy to become the most popular brand national restaurant chain. At that time, I suggested to my brother that was the first thing we need to agree on. He accepted without thinking. Then it all started. We agreed to spend and reinvest all the profit from the coming five years in the development of the company.

After having decided the budgets, I started working on the planning and allocating the budget. Then I made the second most important decision when I decided to invest in quality of service, interior and packaging of our products. Some solutions were expensive, and some just a clever idea to solve a certain issue. I am a perfectionist. I spent 15 years thinking about the idea and now it was true, everything had to be perfect. I did not tolerate anything but perfection. Those were extremely stressful years for me, and most probably for the employees too. There were periods full of problems and the solving of problems in terms of standardization, quality, organization, re-organization, packing, productivity, in-store branding, quality and speed of service, innovative products, innovative services, innovative methods of work, etc.

I don't regret having any of the thousands of problems that occurred and which I solved. The problems suddenly made our service and products perfect, and customers appreciated our final output. Of course, everything I did was based on concept, system and cause-effect development, in line with enhancing customer experiences. Very few people could smell the concept behind which I was cooking. My parents were not among them.

Within the first year of implementing these ideas, we experienced 30% growth while we decreased costs by 20%. We served more customers with lower costs. That was an excellent result!

It was just a beginning. One day, soon after the concept and system changes took effect, I received a call from the most popular business magazine that asked to have a cup of coffee with me. I was surprised and decided to see this journalist for a short meeting in our restaurant. He informed me that his field of expertise was marketing, and he wanted to have an interview with me and report it on two full pages free of charge! Why? Because he recognized the potential of our efforts in the restaurant, and wanted to be the first to publish something about us. Of course I accepted, and he made a great story for our brand and products, presenting it as a world class brand (no wonder, it really looked like that in terms of quality and packaging, but far from the size of marketing budgets and efforts that international brands have). It had a great response, as it was the most popular business newspaper, and several other newspapers published similar stories after that.

People started loving what we offered and how we offered it. I started to receive congrats almost every day. As the image was growing and more and more customers were happy, customer references and appreciation was increasing, and they became our best marketing asset. Very soon, people and customers from other cities, predominantly from the capital, started to ask us to open a shop in their cities – simply by writing on our email, social media, blogs etc. Of course, we were happy to hear that and finally decided to open a shop in the nation's capital city.

We selected the best location in the city center on the most frequented passenger street in the city. Again, we decided not to invest in marketing but in the restaurant itself, and in the quality of everything you can imagine inside—the best professional equipment in the industry at that time, creative interior design, the best sound equipment, the best air quality system, heating, cooling, playlists with carefully-selected artists, a library, a gallery, decibel meters for loudness, new innovative cakes and other products—and finally we made a contract with the world's best coffee brand and started to serve it for the first time in the city. We wanted to offer an experience that had never been seen in the city and the country before.

And then reconstruction of the place began. We dismantled everything inside and outside the shop and rebuilt it according to our standards and our vision. The whole renovation process by itself attracted a lot of buzz as it happened on the busiest street in the city. As we covered the store with the logos of our brands and with "Opening on …" text, the buzz on the Internet and in the newspapers started dramatically. By next day, all the Internet news portals were writing about the opening of their favorite restaurant brand in their capital city. And then the opening day finally arrived. It was an opening with a queue of hundreds of people waiting for the opening of the shop. Until then, I had seen similar examples only on the world's best brands launching some high-tech products, and people waiting on the shop to open to be among the first to buy the product. It was absolutely the same! The buzz lasted for months.

Most of the business people I met then, and for months and months after the opening, they congratulated me for the best PR they ever saw. All the newspapers, TV shows, radio shows, tweets, jokes in newspapers, etc., were writing and talking about the opening of the restaurant or mentioning the name in different contexts. It was the best PR and marketing I've had managed up to that time, and it cost me no money at all.

Guests were amazed by the interior, environment, new products, world's best coffee, etc. And they continued to appreciate and visit our store. Soon after the opening, we launched an Internet profile on the most popular social network. Within a week, we had more than 30,000 fans without needing any software tools or models to generate fans, or to do marketing activities to generate more fans from concepts like: "if you want to read this, please register or be a fan." It was a great experience, from which I have learned what the key to guerrilla success is, and without doing any marketing investment. So, based on my experiences, these are my seven steps of Guerrilla Success concepts that will cost you no marketing investment. Use them, and customers will do the marketing for you, free of charge.

THE SEVEN STEPS OF GUERRILLA SUCCESS CONCEPTS

1. Create excellent quality service or product (in your opinion, you have to start from somewhere)
2. Understand the micro and macro environment
3. Understand the system you are in and its laws of behavior, connectivity and cause/effect rules
4. Connect your product or service to the system
5. Watch how customers are reacting
6. Check if points 1, 2 and 3 are still matching
7. Eliminate differences and continue from point 4 again

*** *** ***

As I think about past experiences with similar effective guerrilla success – without any investment in marketing – I remember almost ten years ago when I started up my first sole business company for providing sales and logistic services. I believed that I could save 2% for the vendors if they decided to use our service. Now after ten years, the company still lives the same mission "to lower the logistic costs for clients by 2% while offering excellence in service and distribution." All this became true because back at that time and even now, I believe that everything which is a problem now, is an opportunity for the future, so I started to solve the problems in sales and logistics in the country and for our first vendors.

They were not day-to-day solutions, but more systematic solutions, like software upgrades and improvements every day, every month, every year. I studied the problem scientifically and conceptually, and analyzed all the aspects, then tried to find a mathematical calculation to prove the solution. Finally, I tested a real life situation in the field. Small solutions were found every day, bigger ones several times a year, and all were added to our company procedures and behavior. Clients began to appreciate our company and our people, and vendor sales started to grow year after year. There were vendors that were leaders in the industry and we have grown their sales ever since. I founded the company with two employees in a small garage warehouse and now it is a company with four Distribution Centers nationwide and serves morc than 3,000 loyal clients every year on an everyday basis, and now it is a seven-digit business heading to become an eight.

In the very first years, the company was not popular in the nation. Several people knew about the company and the services, but were sceptical. The quality of service was a must, our focus was strong, and I really did not have the time to look at what was going on above and beyond logistics. Then years were passing, we were still growing with a lot of hands-on work. Then suddenly, after six to seven years of good quality work, I received mail that stated that we are in the group of fastest growing companies in the nation, with double-digit growth rates five years or so in a row. I had never thought of comparing the results more than to the previous year, and I knew that we were growing, but I never thought it was enough! Suddenly we were the fastest-growing company! Our peers in the industry either declined or their growth was very limited. Then from the well-respected news magazine in the nation, again I was asked to give an interview about how we managed to grow by double-digit growth rates in an economy that was stable or in some years even declining (it was during the world economic crises). That is how it happened for my company to receive huge PR about its services and helped to expand its business further.

*** *** ***

Another very important issue I always teach my employees and people that ask for advice from me is that you always need to give more to the client than what they expected. When you give, you need to give more, and after that again more, and so on. You must be creative to find ways to positively surprise your clients. The relationship needs to grow all the time and you are responsible for it to happen! Your clients are the best and most valuable marketing tool, so never let them down, and never put your short-term interest ahead of the long term. Speaking about long term, it's only fair-play that lasts forever, and builds bridges and bonds of steel between seller and client. Their references and happiness from your service or product are a far more efficient tool than the most successful marketing or advertising strategy.

Very often, I am asked how can I have strong business growth in the short term without having to spend a lot of money to acquire a certain company that is compatible and worth acquiring? I tell them there are several options to achieve that. First, you dedicate yourself in line with your mission and identify relationships of potential mutual benefits. Then try to understand their problem, find solutions for their problem, give them a test product or service for free or your best price. Be sure that you can benefit from the solution too. Finally, offer them your service/product and make a business partnership with strong bonds of mutual interest. . . and be loyal all the time.

Looking back at the two guerrilla success stories, I identified behaviors that were key to their success. There are five guerrilla success behavior pieces of advice that every successful entrepreneur needs to adopt.

THE FIVE GUERRILLA SUCCESS BEHAVIORS TO ADOPT

1. Be mission-driven, don't be result-driven.
2. Never give up, repeat and improve.
3. Working hard is not enough, you need to work smart too. Don't forget, I said work hard first.
4. Adopt a mindset to have a problem-solving attitude. Not only attitude, solve the problems!
5. Limits are only in your head. There are no limits in the outside world. I said limits are in the head, so they exist. Work on your limits and extend your mind's capabilities and knowledge.

About Igor

Igor Nikoloski is an international multi-industry marketing expert, creator, conceptualist and entrepreneur. He is founder and CEO of several international companies, owner and co-owner of many brands in several industries. Currently, Igor is President of the board of his family's national restaurant chain business, and co-owner of many brands in the FMCG. Igor also serves as a managing director of Total Brands Ltd. for Central and Southeastern Europe.

Two years ago he launched *gute FRÜCHTE* (a juice brand), and reached 95% brand awareness in the first year of launch, and made it one of the most popular juice brands in his country within two years from launch. Igor is famous for his efficient and practical extraordinary guerrilla marketing strategies. He is founder and CEO at Total Logistic Ltd. Igor is happily married to Katerina and they have one child.

Skype: i.nikoloski
E-mail: i.nikoloski@total-logistic.com

CHAPTER 5

SAFEGUARDING YOUR MISSION

BY JW DICKS & NICK NANTON

A study pegged him as the 23rd most trustworthy person in the nation.

Which was good, because he needed to be trustworthy. Every weeknight, he spent the better part of a half hour telling an audience of 19 million people the events of the day. Without that belief in his honesty and integrity in place…well, who would listen to him? After ten years serving as network anchor, he had become the dominant news person on the air as well as the face of the network's news operation. And because of his proven success, towards the end of 2014, he was given a new five-year contract, reportedly paying him $10 million a year. He was clearly at the top of his game.

But, just a few weeks later, all that would change.

On January 30th, 2015, Brian Williams paid tribute to a veteran on the NBC Nightly News, saying the man had helped protect him when the helicopter Williams was in was hit by an RPG. When that was posted on Facebook, another veteran commented, "Sorry dude, I don't remember you being on my aircraft. I do remember you walking up about an hour after we had landed to ask me what had happened." The military newspaper Stars and Stripes reported on the comment and soon there was talk everywhere that Brian Williams had exaggerated the incident and put himself in a damaged helicopter, when he was in fact riding in a different one.

It didn't take long for Williams to note the controversy and understand that it had to be addressed. On February 4th, he formally apologized for his mistake both on Facebook and on the nightly news, saying it was the "fog of memory" that had caused him to "conflate" the two helicopters.

He had hoped that would be the end – but, in reality, it was only just the beginning.

Soon, a clip from two years earlier of Williams on the David Letterman Show began popping up on Facebook and Twitter – a clip in which he described in dramatic detail what happened when the helicopter he was riding in was hit by enemy fire, a story that wasn't true. That raised more questions and the media began poking around at other of his claims over the years. Suddenly, his reporting on Hurricane Katrina was rendered suspicious, as were his remarks about being at the Berlin Wall when it came down or about being embedded with Seal Team 6 on top secret missions.

On January 30th, Brian Williams was the 23rd most trusted person in America. On February 9th, he was down to the 835th. And one day later, on February 10th, NBC announced it was suspending Brian Williams for 6 months – without pay.

News gathering, whether it's for print, television, radio or Internet, is by definition heavily Mission-Driven. Its specific mission requires the organization behind it to maintain the highest standards of journalism and integrity, or the public will quickly turn its back on it. It's no different when it comes to business, as we're about to explain in this exclusive excerpt from our new best-selling book, *Mission-Driven Business.*

THE IMPACT OF MISSION FAILURE

The advantages of being a business being successfully mission-driven are myriad and powerful; when people believe in what you're doing, they will reward you with a loyalty that goes beyond what usually accompanies simply providing a good product or service. This, however, also leads to one deep downside for the Mission-Driven organization or even, as evidenced by Brian Williams, the Mission-Driven individual. When you are seen to betray the mission that so many entrust you with, the anger and rejection can be swift, brutal and overwhelming. Because you are connected to the public on a higher level that supersedes "business as usual," you are also held to a higher standard of conduct.

Research verifies the catastrophic results that can occur when a brand seemingly betrays that higher standard. Economic reporter Brad Tuttle puts it this way: "Experts who study marketing and company-consumer relationships believe that brands that have developed cult-like followings for supposedly doing things the right and honorable way—Chipotle and Whole Foods come to mind—are likely to feel greater backlash if and when they appear to violate customers' trust." Tuttle goes on to make the point that consumers expect the worst from monolithic businesses such as banks and cable companies – which is why they expect so much more from Mission-Driven ones.

One Mission-Driven business that has flirted uncomfortably close with mission failure in recent months is Uber. Among the accusations that have been leveled at the company are:
- Threatening to investigate the private lives of journalists who write critical pieces about the company
- Employing less-than-safe or less-than-savory drivers
- Invading the privacy of users of the service
- Using hardball tactics to threaten competing services

How do all these less-than-admirable tactics threaten Uber's mission – which is simply to get people to their destinations?

The New York Times answers that question very effectively - "Uber and its investors believe that the company's long-term mission is to reinvent transportation, to become not just a taxi service but also a replacement for private cars. That mission can be realized only if people trust the company implicitly and automatically."

POWERING PAST THE PITFALLS OF MISSION-DRIVEN BUSINESSES

What does it take to really sink a Mission-Driven business – or, at the very least, substantially diminish its success? Let's look at five big pitfalls that too often threaten companies that promote their purposes – and how to ensure you survive them.

- **Pitfall #1: Changing the Mission at the Expense of Your Customer**

  It may be impossible to believe now, but there was a brief moment in 2011 when streaming powerhouse Netflix looked as though it was a goner, due to an almost-fatal self-inflicted wound.

  Netflix had basically bankrupted Blockbuster by making movie rentals by mail easy, automatic and affordable – no late fees and no late-night trips to the store to make a return. At the same time, Netflix had its eyes on the future; they didn't want to get blindsided by technology the way Blockbuster had, so they started a streaming service which DVD subscribers received as part of their monthly fee. It took off quickly. In 2010, within a matter of months, the company went from being the postal service's number one customer to becoming the biggest source of Internet traffic. They correctly saw that streaming was where their business would ultimately end up and, in October 2011, they announced they were spinning off their DVD service into a separate company so they could purely focus on their Internet offerings.

What seemed like a sound business decision felt like betrayal by its customers, who suddenly had to pay almost twice as much for the same DVD/streaming combo package they had had in the past. Result? Netflix lost a million customers within a month, its stock price fell by 19%, and it had to announce in November of 2011 that at the end of 2012, over a full year away, the company would still be unprofitable.

The fact is that, even though changing up its strategy was the smart move, the abrupt left turn was too much for its customers to handle at once. The company ended up reversing course a month later and canceled plans to spin off the DVD rentals into a separate enterprise. Subscriber anger cooled and soon, the company roared back stronger than ever.

How to Power Past this Pitfall

There's certainly more long-term danger in not changing up a business mission when necessary. Netflix had only to look at the ruins of Blockbuster to see what happened when you failed to keep up with technology in the marketplace. But Netflix was too anxious to avoid the mistakes of its predecessor – it not only abandoned its core business too quickly, it also made the mistake of increasing the cost of the service its customers were getting by an alarming 67%. None of the temporary and traumatic losses Netflix suffered were necessary – they just tried to do too much too soon.

Instead, when you are in the midst of changing missions, make it a lengthy transition – and make your customer base feel as little of the pain as possible. Don't inconvenience them or overcharge them for a changeover that's your responsibility to pull off – or they'll resent you for making your problem *their* problem. And if you too do too much too fast, take a page from Netflix's playbook, reverse course and make amends to your customers.

- **Pitfall #2: Pursuing an Outdated Mission**

This was the pitfall Netflix was trying to avoid when it ran into the other one instead – that's because this one can mean a complete dead-end for your company. Times change, cultures change, and technology changes – and if your organizational mission doesn't change as well, what brought you huge success in the past might bring you nothing but misery in the future. Remember that in 1976, Kodak owned 90% of the photography market – and in 2012, it filed for bankruptcy. What happened in between was the introduction of digital technology that made the buying and processing of camera film completely unnecessary.

How to Power Past this Pitfall
Both Blockbuster and Kodak had many opportunities to adapt to changing times – but both did too little too late. When a company owns a certain sector of an industry, it all too easily can fall into complacency, believing its dominance will weather any storm.
That's why it's important to continually analyze your business mission in terms of changing times – and ask questions such as:
- *Is our mission still relevant?*
- *Is the marketplace changing in such a way as to render us obsolete?*
- *Are consumers beginning to view us as old-fashioned and out of step?*
- *Is someone else fulfilling our mission in a newer, more efficient and/or more exciting way?*

One needs only to look at the contrasting examples of Apple and Microsoft to see how two huge Mission-Driven companies can respond to these questions quite differently – and achieve quite different results. While Apple easily morphed from being primarily a computer company to a music company to a smartphone company, all while keeping their mission solidly in place, Microsoft remains anchored to its Windows operating system as well as its Office software. While it's taken a stab at creating its own versions of music players, smartphones, video game consoles, etc., it frankly hasn't gotten very far from where it started. And, let's remember, even Windows was a direct "borrowing" of Apple's original Macintosh operating system.

Continually updating and evolving your mission is a necessity, not an option. If your mission isn't moving forward, it's probably falling behind.

- **Pitfall #3: Diluting Your Mission**

JetBlue was founded in 1998 with a very distinct mission in place. That mission was, in the words of founder David Neeleman, "to bring humanity back to air travel," and was fulfilled by charging less than the big airlines but, at the same time, offering such extra amenities as a TV at every seat. It became so successful that other airlines tried (and failed) to emulate it.

However, after a few years, JetBlue ran up against some strong headwinds from the marketplace. As other airlines' began to see their profits soar, JetBlue's remained stagnant. Wall Street analysts began attacking the CEO as being "overly concerned' with passengers and their comfort, which they feel, has come at the expense of shareholders." The new CEO, not overly concerned that the airline built its brand on a customer-friendly philosophy, began adding more seats to planes, increasing crowding, and charging more for snacks and luggage, increasing the expense to its fliers.

That, of course, upset those customers who were faithful to the company because of its mission. As CNN Money put it, "…it's clear that the values originally embraced by the brand have changed as well. For the people who loved and were loyal to JetBlue specifically because of its egalitarian, customers-first approach, the latest moves serve as a big slap in the face."

The company, at least in its press releases, remains committed to a customer-first approach. Its current president claims that "JetBlue's core mission to Inspire Humanity and its differentiated model of serving underserved customers remain unchanged." But, while fliers can still enjoy that TV at their seat, many who once swore by the airline will now undoubtedly shop around for the best-priced ticket instead of the most convenient JetBlue flight.

How to Power Past this Pitfall
Perhaps JetBlue did have to make those tweaks to its business in order to keep the company healthy. But it could have found other ways to deal with the situation rather than just announce it was still committed to its original mission and then demonstrate the opposite. There are few things worse than talking incessantly about your mission at the same time you're scaling back on it; all the trust you took so much time building with your fanbase is immediately eroded. That's because actions speak louder than words – and when the actions directly contradict the words, your public image takes a big hit.
So what should JetBlue have done?

First of all, it should have been honest about why it was doing what it was doing, instead of pretending its mission was still firmly in place. Instead of trumpeting its concern for its passengers, JetBlue should have said it was regretful that these moves were necessary.

Second of all, JetBlue should have found some ways to sweeten customer experience in more cost-effective ways. Maybe a free snack or additional loyalty program bonuses

– something that would have been a significant gesture of good will to frequent customers who would feel the pain of the economizing.

Finally, they should have heeded a piece of advice we offered earlier in this chapter: *Don't change too quickly*. Rather than do a whole bunch of things that significantly detract from the fliers' experience, maybe just do one at a time over a longer period. When everything gets bad at once, people really stand up and take notice – and immediately come to the conclusion that everything about your business is going south.

• Pitfall #4: Violating Your Customers' Values

In 1998, Lululemon was founded to provide upscale yoga-fitness apparel for women. The company was a huge success and, a few years later, it was earning over a billion dollars in revenue. However, its founder, Chip Wilson, generated a lot of controversy with his outspoken ways. For example, he stated that he named the company "Lululemon" because it was hard for Japanese people to say, so they would have to make an extra effort when marketing it in their country. "It's funny to watch them try and say it," explained Wilson. He also talked approvingly about child labor in developing countries and claimed that birth control pills led to high divorce rates.

He really began to get in trouble when he said his company doesn't make clothes for plus-size women because it costs too much money. And he also blamed excessive pilling in Lululemon pants on that segment of the buying public as well, saying "Frankly some women's bodies just don't actually work for it...it's really about the rubbing through the thighs, how much pressure is there over a period of time, how much they use it."

The remarks in the above paragraph caused the company's stock value to plummet by a third – and forced Wilson to resign as Lululemon CEO.

Now, none of what Wilson said had anything to do with the company's actual business practices, products or fulfillment of its stated mission. But what his remarks did do is *offend* the sensibilities of his main target group – women. He violated their values loudly and without restraint and caused tremendous damage to the brand.

How to Power Past this Pitfall
An organization's management must be careful with public remarks and their own personal actions. If a representative of a company says or does the wrong thing, it immediately causes negative repercussions throughout social media.

That's why *control* is so important to a Mission-Driven business. It has to be careful who it hires, which vendors it does business with and what its own leaders say and do, both behind closed doors and in the public spotlight.

When this kind of mishap does occur, however, a sincere apology should come quickly and steps should immediately be taken to compensate for the damage (a big charitable contribution to a relevant cause, for example). Sometimes this isn't enough, however, and the person involved must be let go – even when, in the case of Lululemon, it's the guy who started the business in the first place!

- **Pitfall #5: Violating the Mission**

For 31 years, Sharper Image sold high-end electronic gadgets designed to appeal to men with a lot of disposable income – and became a familiar sight in most of America's malls. But in 2002, Consumer Reports published a report that stated one of Sharper Image's air purifier products didn't do such a great job of purifying the air – as a matter of fact, the magazine said that the purifier released unhealthy levels of ozone into the space it occupied.

In other words, it did the exact opposite of what it was supposed to do. Sharper Image tried to sue Consumer Reports for libel. The suit was dismissed, and soon the company was forced to accept massive amounts of returns on the product, including units that were many years old.

The merchant finally ended up filing for bankruptcy in 2008.

There is no bleaker scenario for a Mission-Driven company than to actually end up doing the opposite of what it sets out to do. JetBlue flirted with that scenario, but Sharper Image took it all the way by not only releasing an unhealthy healthy product, but defending it even when it shouldn't have. The resulting controversy not only cost the company millions of dollars in returns and lost sales, but also broke trust with the public.

How to Power Past this Pitfall

When something serious happens to derail your mission, you must take swift action and do whatever it takes to restore trust. That can mean doing things that seem to be insanely overboard – but it's better to do too much than what will be perceived to be too little by the public.

The corporation behind the pain reliever Tylenol wrote the book on dealing with this most difficult of situations way back in 1982, when several of their pills were tampered with on supermarket shelves in Chicago – and ended up killing seven people. As in the case of The Sharper Image, a product the public trusted to improve their health actually threatened it.

To deal with the situation, Johnson & Johnson, the Tylenol manufacturer, ended up recalling ALL Tylenol products from ALL across the nation at a cost of over $100 million. In the process, they saved a threatened brand and earned plaudits for their extensive action. As *The Washington Post* put it at the time, "Johnson & Johnson has effectively demonstrated how a major business ought to handle a disaster."

When you do the opposite of what you promise, it threatens your very viability as an organization. Therefore, no action is too extreme to make things right again.

As you can see from what we've discussed in this chapter, a mission can be a very fragile commodity. But it doesn't have to be. If you remain true to your stated objectives and consistent in implementing them throughout your business practices, your mission should grow and thrive along with your profits. If, however, you ignore or take your mission for granted and fail to live up to its requirements, what could have been one of your greatest assets could end up to be your greatest weakness.

About JW

JW Dicks Esq., is a Wall Street Journal Best-Selling Author®, Emmy Award-Winning Producer, publisher, board member, and advisor to organizations such as the XPRIZE, The National Academy of Best-Selling Authors®, and The National Association of Experts, Writers and Speakers®.

JW is the CEO of DNAgency and is a strategic business development consultant to both domestic and international clients. He has been quoted on business and financial topics in national media such as the *USA Today, The Wall Street Journal, Newsweek, Forbes, CNBC.com,* and *Fortune Magazine Small Business.*

Considered a thought leader and curator of information, JW has more than forty-three published business and legal books to his credit and has co-authored with legends like Brian Tracy, Jack Canfield, Tom Hopkins, Dr. Nido Qubein, Dr. Ivan Misner, Dan Kennedy, and Mari Smith. He is the resident branding expert for Fast Company's Internationally-syndicated blog and is the editor and publisher of the *Celebrity Expert Insider,* a monthly newsletter sent to experts worldwide.

JW is called the "Expert to the Experts" and has appeared on business television shows airing on ABC, NBC, CBS, and FOX affiliates around the country. His co-produced television series, *Profiles of Success,* appears on the Bio Channel - along with other branded films he has produced. JW also co-produces and syndicates a line of franchised business television shows and received an Emmy Award as Executive Producer of the film, *Mi Casa Hogar.*

JW and his wife of forty-two years, Linda, have two daughters, three granddaughters, and two Yorkies. He is a sixth generation Floridian and splits his time between his home in Orlando and his beach house on Florida's west coast.

About Nick

An Emmy Award-Winning Director and Producer, Nick Nanton, Esq., is known as the Top Agent to Celebrity Experts around the world for his role in developing and marketing business and professional experts, through personal branding, media, marketing and PR. Nick is recognized as the nation's leading expert on personal branding as *Fast Company Magazine's* Expert Blogger on the subject and lectures regularly on the topic at major universities around the world. His book *Celebrity Branding You®*, while an easy and informative read, has also been used as a text book at the University level.

The CEO and Chief StoryTeller at The Dicks + Nanton Celebrity Branding Agency, an international agency with more than 1800 clients in 33 countries, Nick is an award-winning director, producer and songwriter who has worked on everything from large scale events to television shows with the likes of Steve Forbes, Brian Tracy, Jack Canfield *(The Secret, Creator of the Chicken Soup for the Soul Series),* Michael E. Gerber, Tom Hopkins, Dan Kennedy and many more.

Nick is recognized as one of the top thought-leaders in the business world and has co-authored 30 best-selling books alongside Brian Tracy, Jack Canfield, Dan Kennedy, Dr. Ivan Misner (Founder of BNI), Jay Conrad Levinson (Author of the Guerrilla Marketing Series), Super Agent Leigh Steinberg and many others, including the breakthrough hit *Celebrity Branding You!®*.

Nick has led the marketing and PR campaigns that have driven more than 1000 authors to Best-Seller status. Nick has been seen in *USA Today, The Wall Street Journal, Newsweek, BusinessWeek, Inc. Magazine, The New York Times, Entrepreneur® Magazine, Forbes, FastCompany.com* and has appeared on ABC, NBC, CBS, and FOX television affiliates around the country, as well as on CNN, FOX News, CNBC, and MSNBC from coast to coast.

Nick is a member of the Florida Bar, holds a JD from the University of Florida Levin College Of Law, as well as a BSBA in Finance from the University of Florida's Warrington College of Business. Nick is a voting member of The National Academy of Recording Arts & Sciences (NARAS, Home to The GRAMMYs), a member of The National Academy of Television Arts &

Sciences (Home to the Emmy Awards), co-founder of the National Academy of Best-Selling Authors, a 16-time Telly Award winner, and spends his spare time working with Young Life, Downtown Credo Orlando, Entrepreneurs International and rooting for the Florida Gators with his wife Kristina and their three children, Brock, Bowen and Addison.

Learn more at: www.NickNanton.com
and: www.CelebrityBrandingAgency.com

CHAPTER 6

ONE SIZE DOESN'T FIT ALL
– HOW TO GET PAID FOR WHAT YOU KNOW

BY ANITA PLAK SEMPRIMOZNIK

WHAT IS THIS CHAPTER ABOUT?

After years of researching different online business models, and what successful experts are doing to make millions online, I came to the conclusion that there are few online business models that work really well. In this chapter I'm going to show you the profitable business model that can turn your passion to profit. And to show those of you who are already selling your knowledge, the way to stop trading your time for money.

The fact is, people are looking for knowledge online. They want to know what to do, how to do it, how to deal with their challenges – whether personally or professionally – or simply want to learn about something they're passionate about. And they're prepared to pay for it, sometimes at a premium.

There is a model which is a great opportunity for all of you who want to share your knowledge with other people, to improve their lives or businesses. It will also work for those who want some freedom and balance in their daily lives.

WHY DO I BELIEVE IN THIS?

At some point, I realised that my passion is to help people become successful with the business of their dreams.

Over the last decade of working with clients, I also realised that people really need and appreciate my coaching and mentoring. And that no matter what services I provide, they'll still need my guidance if they want to achieve great results.

There have also been some instances that I had a greater desire for my clients to succeed than they did themselves. At that point I realised that I was working for the wrong type of clients. They were just draining my energy, asking for free advice, but never did their part properly – until I had enough and stopped it. I learned some great lessons in the process.

I cannot imagine working for the rest of my life by providing just services and trading my time for money. I have a limited amount of time per month. So I needed to figure out how to do less for more, and get paid for what I know—a business that I'll be passionate about.

Remember: Ideas don't work without you doing the work.
~ author unknown

WHERE TO START?

You may be asking yourself: Why should I consider this business model? What is the opportunity? What can I offer or teach people?

The heart of your business may be something you're very familiar with and good at, i.e., your current profession. Or you're so passionate about a certain topic or hobby that you're already spending hours learning all about it or even doing it for yourselves.

Just imagine if you go for a coffee with some friends – what are they asking you to help them with? What are you an expert at? Or what passion or hobby do you usually talk about? We all have something inside us that we can help other people or their businesses with. You just need to explore it and start turning it into a profitable business, following the first steps I'm about to teach you.

There are many coaches and mentors who are devoted to their clients and producing great results, however they're not making a lot of money out of it. Why? Simply because they offer their services in exchange for pay for their time, rather than for the value they provide or by exploiting a unique online business model. So how can they stretch their effort, their time? How to make more money out of it? The answer is simply by taking a certain part of their knowledge and services online. And start selling one-to-many rather than one-to-one. For example, if you are already offering training courses, put them in a digital form. If you provide services or coaching or consulting, think what are the steps, activities or questions that you encounter in every process with every client. Those are excellent to package into the digital product and sell online. You may also consider obtaining knowledge through research or by performing interviews with the top experts from a selected field, and packaging it into a digital product. The opportunities are endless.

Then you can automate your business and sell the digital product while you sleep. You can still provide certain services offline or in the way you feel is most appropriate for you and your clients. However, now you have the freedom to reduce the number of hours you spend one-on-one, or you charge more per hour, or you simplify the whole process of serving clients. For example, instead of coaching one-to-one, try and consolidate the same type of clients into group coaching. Or create live events once or twice per year. And then you can charge much higher hourly rates, as you have only a minimum amount of time available for one-on-one sessions. So you may choose to work in person just with the high-end clients or clients you really resonate with.

We should never underestimate the importance of the process and the content (message) when implementing marketing strategies and tactics. That is why guerrilla marketing is so powerful. It teaches us to put in our time, energy and focus on the target clients that we really care for, whilst executing activities towards achieving the maximum profit.

THE CORE MODEL – THE BASICS

As in every business and learning cycle, there are basic, intermediate and advanced levels. In this chapter I will touch on the basics. Basics will remain the same throughout the different levels of sophistication. What differentiates the levels are the refining of the strategies and tactics, refining details within the process, creating complexity in offering, fine tuning of the sales funnels and promotions, and narrowing down the messages that clients will resonate with, etc. Learn and grow step by step. And apply what you learn on the go!

CHOOSE THE TOPIC-CONTENT – Select the topic you want to be in. Perform some research on the Internet and check whether some people are already selling products under this topic. More competition means greater opportunity. Check in at your favorite search engine and check on most popular affiliate network sites, other websites and forums, and see what people like the most in that niche. Check and review what are the topics, comments and replies.

DEFINE THE CLIENT AVATAR – Define who is your perfect client. What are their characteristics. Find out what they really want to learn, what are their challenges, pain points, hot buttons, objections, etc. Then offer them a digital product on that topic to provide them valuable solutions to their challenges.

CREATE THE PRODUCT – Create the first simple product for sales. Also create the digital information product that you'll offer for free (for example: e-books, cheat sheets, info research, how to's, tool sets, tips and tricks, etc.). Once the first product is in the profit generation "pipeline," start working on creating different products at different price points. Such products could be online training courses, monthly subscription programs, online group coaching, teleseminars, webinars, e-books or books.

CREATE AN APPEALING MESSAGE – Based on your client avatar definition and the research findings, crafting the message is a very important task. You need to explain what value you're providing to clients, address their objections and explain all the benefits they're getting. You must be a solution for their problem! They need to understand what you expect them to do and what's in it for them. The focus must be on them, not you! This applies to all the content in each of your communication channels.

CREATE A SQUEEZE PAGE – This is also an essential part of the profit generation cycle. Use modern tools to setup a landing page – a one-page website with an opt-in form. You may use the combination of text and images or create a video sales letter. But in both cases, you must include an opt-in form.

BUILD AN EMAIL LIST – Start collecting emails. Whether on your landing page or any other digital asset, you must have an opt-in form to start collecting emails – where potential clients will give you their email for exchange for the download of the free digital information product (e-book, cheat sheet, info research, how to's, tool sets, tips & tricks, etc.). Connect the opt-in form with the emailing platform for sending blast emails. Having an email list is your essential asset for the ongoing profit generation.

SETUP A SALES FUNNEL – Start with the basic one. Use existing tools on the market, preferably with an easy payment option. Drive people to your opt-in page and offer them a free product for the exchange of their email address. On the "thank you" page, where they get the free product, offer them another product that you're selling. You may also create another product for upsell – what you'll offer them next – another product, advanced version of the training, group coaching session, membership sites, etc. Ideally, you would have it at the beginning, however you can add it at any later stage. The earlier you setup a more advanced sales funnel, the bigger the profit opportunity.

PROMOTE YOUR OFFER – There are many ways to promote your offer. The most common are different type of ads, JV's (joint promotions), sending emails to your list and appointing affiliate marketers to help you promote your offer. Keep promoting. Remember: people only buy what's in front of them.

PUT THE BUSINESS ON AUTOPILOT – Create advanced sales funnels supported by the traffic (ads, blogs, affiliates, JV's, and so on). Automate email responses and email communication cycles. Offer your product on affiliate sites, so that other people will promote and sell it for you. You only pay them a commission after they make a sale.

GET A COACH OR MENTOR – Let them guide you through the process.

KEEP LEARNING AND GROWING – Learning should never stop. My advice to you is learn from the best. Learn from people who have done it. If you study them long enough, you'll notice they're still learning. That is what is keeping them on the edge. There are quite a number of experts (or their legacies) that can teach you specifics and advanced techniques of each step. Therefore, keep learning—not just about the elements of this business model, but also keep working on your personal growth.

Given that this book should remain evergreen, I intentionally haven't mentioned specific tools or portals as those may change over time. Instead, for the purpose of further supporting you, the reader of my book, I will maintain additional info. and resources on my website, which I have added at the end of my biography.

TIPS ON HOW TO DEAL WITH THE OBJECTIONS YOU MIGHT HAVE WHILST DECIDING IF THIS IS THE RIGHT BUSINESS MODEL FOR YOU

Don't get distracted or let others discourage you from your ideas by the cliché that other people are already doing that, or there are better experts than I am and so on. It's even good, as this is proof to you that the niche you're dreaming about actually exists, and some people are making a fortune out of it. The second thing is that we cannot work with everybody. It's not that some of them are good or bad. We select a coach, mentor, trainer or business partner with whom we like and feel energetically connected. In other words, we like them and they like us. Or maybe we share the same values. Remember, there are more potential clients on this planet than there are professionals that can serve them.

Don't overthink it and don't be overwhelmed by the methods to get there. There are many trainings, books, mentors or coaches that can show you the way. And there are many people you can outsource to do the techy part on your behalf. Therefore, rather focus on who those people are that you can help, to solve their challenges by what you already know and you're passionate about.

Don't be scared about the "how" part, especially the technical side. And don't be overwhelmed by all those activities. Simply focus and make the first step.

Don't lose time by waiting for your digital asset to get perfected. Start immediately and then add better versions onboard. You'll be making money whilst preparing the higher-priced digital product. This may be also great motivation to complete it asap, as you'll see the first results coming in.

Don't look at the whole picture and get overwhelmed. Of course you need to have a clear picture of the end result in mind. However, don't get stuck by questioning how to get there or look for excuses as to why to start or even worse, to quit. Rather, take the simple approach. Slice down the activities, put them in the right order and take action on them step-by-step. Then you start looking into which activities you can do yourself and which ones you'll need to either outsource or find additional info or help to perform.

CONCLUSION

Each of us has certain knowledge to share with other people. Don't waste your talent. Show it to the world. Create your legacy. I showed you how and where to start. Now it's up to you. I really wish you succeed. There are some great experts and extraordinary people that I have learned a lot from and who really inspired me.

One was my dear mentor Jay Conrad Levinson, the father of Guerrilla Marketing, that I had the privilege to personally meet and spent some precious time with. Unfortunately, he passed away. However, he left a great legacy that will be with us forever. His Guerrilla marketing techniques can be applied in every marketing activity in every business or business model.

Then, there is Brendon Burchard, one of the top motivation and marketing trainers in the world, that really inspires me. Every time that I listen or watch his trainings, I want more. Not to mention live events that are just the best.

Anik Singal is one of the world's leading authorities in digital publishing. His trainings are really hands-on and are an essential part of this business model.

I'm sure you will find some that you'll get inspired by.

About Anita

Anita Plak Semprimoznik's passion is to help people become successful with the business of their dreams. She chooses to focus on the positive and works with clients that appreciate her advice and are ready to do their part in a timely manner. She's brilliant in discovering people's strengths and their opportunities, personal or business-related.

She is an extremely creative and experienced individual with extensive business background.

Anita is a Digital Marketer and Certified Guerrilla Marketing Coach with over twenty-six years of senior managerial experience. Over half of her career was spent in multinational companies. Her winning combination of Strategic Input, Training, Experience, and Passion is what she has to offer her clients, associates and partners as the first step toward their business profitability.

As a digital marketer, she plays a key role in the successful planning and implementation of multi-channel marketing strategies for client brands.

Learn more about Anita's favorite business model by following her at:
www.experts-valley.com
https://www.linkedin.com/in/aplak

CHAPTER 7

DIALING FOR DOLLARS
– TELEPHONE TECHNIQUES FOR GUERRILLA SUCCESS PRESENTATION PLANNING

BY JAY CONRAD LEVINSON AND
JEANNIE LEVINSON

SUCCESSFUL TELEPHONE TECHNIQUES

Before dialing the phone, savvy telemarketers ask themselves questions like:

- What do I know about the prospect?
- What do I need to know in order for the prospect to take the action desired?
- What information might be obtained from a database or screener?
- What do I say if voice-mail technology answers the call?
- What will my opening statement be?
- What questions will I ask?
- How will I end the call, (no matter what happens)?

Successful Guerrilla Entrepreneurs ask themselves similar questions, and rehearse their telephone techniques.

79

Voice training

No matter who does the calling, proper voice training is a good idea. Talk clearly. Use short sentences. Talk loud enough, but not directly into the mouthpiece; talking across the mouthpiece gives the most effective voice transmission.

Your voice should project authority and warmth while instilling trust. Your message should be stated as concisely as possible.

Script or not to script?

Whatever you do, don't read from a script. However, research shows that it's always a good idea to memorize a script, changing any words that feel awkward or uncomfortable.

The script must be so well memorized that the words sound as though you know them by heart—as natural as the Pledge of Allegiance. Don't use words that feel strange to say. Find words and phrases that come naturally to you. Leave space for the person on the other end to respond.

Guerrillas are in full control of their telemarketing and do not recite awkward speeches to their prospects. Doing so is bad business — more personal than a computer pitch—but still not worth doing if not done right.

Scripts versus outlines

Studies in various industries consistently show that a memorized telemarketing presentation always produces better results than the same presentation from an outline.

You may think it's better to let the caller use his or her own words, but few callers have the ability to summon the right ones. Gone are the days when it was recommended that callers use an outline, or thought-flow.

Still, the more naturally conversant you sound, the more sales you'll make—and that takes practice. Naturally, much of what you
say will be in response to what the person being called says, but the best telemarketers are in full control of the call. They stay in control by asking questions, responding to the answers, then asking more questions, directing the conversation towards the customers getting what they need and a sale being made.

Outline guidelines

If you are still more comfortable using an outline to structure your phone presentations, heed the following guidelines:

- If the outline is longer than one page, there is probably too much in it and you should try to streamline it.

- An outline does create a structure for your thoughts and ideas, and also helps keep the call on track when the person at the other end redirects it.

- Even if you do work from an outline, it's still a good idea to write a script of a phone call.

Working with a script

Once you have written the script, you should do three things with it:
1. Record it.

See what it sounds like. After all, you'll be using "ear" words that are heard, rather than "eye" words that are seen. There's a big, big difference. Words that callers unconsciously love to hear are: profits, sales, dollars, revenues, income, cash flow, savings, time, productivity, morale, motivation, output, attitude, image, victories, market share, and competitive edge.

2. Conversational.

Make sure the recorded script sounds like a conversation and not like an ad. Leave room for the person being called to talk.

3. Rephrase not repeat.

Make it a point not to restate the script but to rephrase it. State the same selling points. Present them in the same order. But use words with which you are comfortable. Your telephone planning should be able to accommodate several situations. After all, if your prospect decides to buy just after you've started, you should be prepared to close the sale and end the conversation.

Analyze yourself

Notice how your friends, and probably even you assume different voice personalities when speaking on the phone. This is subtle, but it's there.

Try to eliminate that telephone personality and bring out your most conversational qualities by actually practicing on the phone—talking to a tape recorder or to a friend.

Role playing

If you're going to do a good amount of telephone marketing, engage in role-playing, with you as the customer and a friend or associate as you. Then switch roles. Role-playing gives you a lot of insight into your offering and your message. Keep doing this until you are completely satisfied with your presentation.

PLANNING YOUR PRESENTATIONS

Asking questions is the best way to prepare a successful presentation

Get in the habit of using the following worksheet to plan your presentations:

Section 1. Purpose

1. What is your message?
2. What does the client want from you?
3. What is your desired outcome from the presentation?
4. What are the client's next steps or actions after the presentation?
5. What information do you need to obtain during the presentation?

Section 2. Resources

6. How much time do you have?
7. Who will be attending?

Section 3. Content

8. What three things do you want your audience to remember?
9. What are your three P's (Purpose, Process and Payoff) for the presentation?
10. What statistics are relevant for this presentation?
11. What gifts can you use in your presentation?
12. What new research or information can you use in this presentation?
13. What questions can you ask them?
14. What creative openers can you use to engage the audience?
15. How can you stretch yourself during this presentation?
16. What exercises can you do to get the point across?
17. How will you end or summarize your presentation?

[Note: For biographical details on the authors, please refer to p.30.]

CHAPTER 8

FACE-TO-FACE SELLING FOR GUERRILLA SUCCESS

BY JAY CONRAD LEVINSON AND
JEANNIE LEVINSON

*See yourself as others see you to help you evaluate and de-
velop rapport, give dynamic presentations and most of all—
close the sale.*

CONTACT

The tone of your meeting is established early. Here are some ways
you can create a positive first impression.

1. Greet your prospect warmly and sincerely, using eye contact.

2. Allow your prospect some time to get acclimated to being
with you, some time to talk. Don't come on too strong. But don't
waste your prospect's time, either.

3. Engage in casual conversation at first—especially about
anything pertinent to your prospect. Make it friendly and not

one-sided. Be a good listener. But, let the prospect know that your time is precious. You are there to sell, not to talk.

4. Ask relevant questions. Listen carefully to the answers.

5. Qualify the prospect. Determine whether or not this is the specific person to whom you should be talking, the person with the authority to give you the go-ahead, to buy.

6. Learn something about the person to whom your contact is directed, so that he or she will feel like a person rather than a prospect. Make your prospect like you, for people enjoy doing business with people they like. The best possible thing you can do is to make your prospect feel unique—proving that you recognize his or her individuality and needs.

7. Be brief, friendly, outgoing, and truly inquisitive. But, be yourself.

8. If you're in a retail environment, one of the best questions to initiate healthy contact is, "Mind if I ask what brings you into our store today?"

9. Don't think of yourself as a salesperson but as a partner to your prospect. This healthy mindset improves both your perspective and your chances of closing. Realize that you have an opportunity to educate your prospects to succeed at whatever they wish to succeed at. As soon as possible, learn what it is that your prospect wishes to succeed at, and then show how what you are selling can make that success achievable.

10. Important elements of your contact are your smile, your attire, your posture, and your willingness to listen and look directly into the prospect's eyes. Your nonverbal communication is as important as your verbal communication. The impression you make will come as much from what you don't say as from what you do say.

YOUR PRESENTATION

When making your presentation, keep in mind that you are not talking by accident. You are there because of intent on your part. If your prospect is still with you, there is intent on his or her part, too. And the intent is to buy.

Either you will buy a story about why a sale cannot be made, or your prospect will buy what you're selling. It truly is up to you. And don't forget: People do enjoy being sold to. They do not like being pressured. They do like being *persuaded* by honest enthusiasm to buy.

The following are some tips to make your presentations flow smoothly and ways to evaluate your technique.

1. List all the benefits of doing business with you, one by one:

The more benefits a prospect knows about, the more likely a prospect will buy. When compiling your list of benefits, invite your employees and at least one customer. Customers are tuned in to benefits you offer that you may take for granted.

2. Emphasize the unique advantages of buying from you:

You should be able to rattle these off with the same aplomb you can state your own name and address. It is upon these competitive advantages that you should be basing your marketing. Don't knock your competition, whatever you do.

3. If your prospect has no experience with what you are selling:

Stress the advantages of your type of offering, then of your specific offering. If you're selling security devices, talk of the value of owning them, then of the value of owning yours.

4. Tailor your presentation:

Tailor your presentation to information learned during your contact. Homework pays off big time to Guerrillas.

5. People do not like to be pioneers:

People do not like to be pioneers because they know darned well that pioneers get arrows in the back of their necks, so mention the acceptance of your products or services by others—especially people in their community. If you can mention names and be specific, by all means do so. The more specific you are, the more closes you'll make. But don't be tedious. You can't bore a prospect into buying.

6. When you know enough about your prospect:

When you know enough about your prospect, you can present your product or service from his or her point of view. This ability will increase your number of closes dramatically. Emphasize what all of your product or service benefits can do for your prospect, not what they can do for the general population.

7. Keep an eagle eye on your prospect's eyes, teeth, and hands:

If the prospect is looking around, rather than at you, you've got to say something to regain attention. If your prospect is not smiling, you are being too serious. Say something to earn a smile. Best of all, smile yourself. That will get your prospect to smile. If your prospect is wringing his or her hands, your prospect is bored. Say something to ease the boredom and spark more interest.

8. A sales point made to the eye:

A sales point made to the eye is 68 percent more effective than one made to the ear. So show as much as you can: photos, drawings, a circular, a product, your sales video, anything. Just be sure it relates to your presentation.

9. Sell the benefit along with the feature:

If the feature is solar power, for instance, the benefit is economy. If the feature is new computer software, the benefit is probably speed or power or profitability.

10. Mention your past successes:

Mention your past successes so the prospect will feel that the key to success is in your hands and there is little chance of a rip-off.

11. Be proud:

Be proud of your prices, proud of your benefits, proud of your offering. Convey your pride with facial expression, tone of voice, and selection of words. Feel the pride and let it come shining through.

There are 250,000 commonly used words in the English language; there are 600,000 nonverbal methods of communications: stance, facial expression, hand gestures, eyebrow position, and 599,996 others. Learn them and utilize them. They're completely free, another example of pure guerrilla marketing. No cost. High payoff.

12. Remain convinced that your prospect will buy from you:

Remain convinced that your prospect will buy from you throughout your presentation. This optimism will be sensed by the prospect and can positively affect the close.

CLOSE

Despite the importance we have attached to the contact and the presentation, we still reiterate that all the marbles are in the close. Effective salespeople and canvassers are effective closers.

Aim to be a "dynamite" closer and your income will reflect this. To close effectively, try to close immediately, rather than in a week or so. Review the tips in the following worksheet and take note of how frequently you utilize the techniques.

1. Always assume that your prospective customer is going to do what you want, so you can close with a leading question such as, "Will it be better for you to take delivery this week or next week?" "Do you want it in gray or brown?"

2. Summarize your main points and confidently end with a closing line such as, "Everything seems to be in order. Why don't I just write up your order now?"

3. Ask the customer to make some kind of decision, and then close on it. Typical points that must be agreed upon are delivery date, size of order, and method of payment. A good closing would be: "I can perform this service for you tomorrow, the eighth, or the fifteenth. The eighth would be best for me. Which would be best for you?"

Begin to attempt the close as soon as possible by easing your prospect into it. If that doesn't work, try again, then again. Continue trying. If you don't, your prospect will spend his or her hard-earned money elsewhere—and with someone else. Count on that.

Remember: People like to be sold to and need to have the deal closed. They won't make the close themselves. So *you are performing a service* when you sell and close.

Always be on the alert for signs that the time is right to close. The prospect will hardly ever tell you when the time has come. You must look for hints in the prospect's words and actions. A mere shifting of weight from one foot to another may be a signal to close.

4. Try to give your prospect a good reason to close immediately. It may be that you won't be back in the neighborhood for a long time, or that the prospect will wish to use your product or service as soon as possible, or that prices are expected to rise, or that you have the time and the inventory now but might not have them later.

5. Let your prospect know of the success of your product or service with people like the prospect, with people recently, with people in the community—people with whom the prospect can easily relate.

6. Be specific with names, dates, costs, times, and benefits. Evasiveness in any area works against you.

7. If the prospect likes what you say, but won't close now, ask, "Why wait?" The prospect may then voice an objection. And you may close by saying, "That's great, and I understand." Then you can solve the objection and close on it. In fact, one of the easiest ways to close is to search for an objection, then solve the problem and close on it.

If you have not yet completed your presentation but feel the time may be right to close, attempt to close on the most important sales point you have yet to state. Always remember that a person knows what you want him or her to do, that there is a reason for your meeting, that your offering does have merit, and that at that moment, your prospect has your offering on his or her mind. Just knowing all these things will make it easier for you to close. When a prospect says "Let me think it over," that means "no."

8. If you do not close after your presentation, chances are you have lost the sale. Few prospects have the guts to tell you they will definitely not buy from you. They search for excuses. So do everything you can to move them into a position where they will buy from you. If you don't, a better salesperson will.

9. Tie the close in with the contact. Try to close on a personal note. Something like, "I think you'll feel more secure now with this new security system, and that's important. Shall I have your smoke alarm installed tomorrow or the next day?"

Guerrilla Marketing involves all aspects of the way you present yourself to clients, customers and prospects. The design of your print and online communications, the appearance and readability of your e-mail messages, the way you respond to telephone calls and your appearance all influence your market's perception of your competence and professionalism.

We have barely scratched the surface of what is "appropriate behavior" for successful Guerrilla Entrepreneurs. Consistently following these suggestions will take you a long way toward projecting a competent, professional image and being the type of person prospects, customers and clients want to be around.

EVALUATING YOUR CUSTOMERS

1. What's a Customer Worth?

Take a minute to determine a critical marketing statistic: "What's the value of each of your customers over his or her lifetime?" Write down the answer and post it over your desk and share it with your employees.

2. Why is this statistic so important?

Because the value of your customers helps you determine how much you might be willing to spend to acquire a new customer. And, just as important, it forces you to realize *how much it costs you to lose a customer once you've got him or her.*

[Note: For biographical details on the authors, please refer to p.30.]

CHAPTER 9

LOOKING GOOD IN PRINT
– GUERRILLA SUCCESS TIPS AND TECHNIQUES FOR ADS, BROCHURES, CARDS MEMOS, NEWSLETTERS AND PROPOSALS

BY JAY CONRAD LEVINSON AND
JEANNIE LEVINSON

The quality of your print communications plays a major role in the way clients and prospects judge your competence and professionalism. "Perception equals reality." If your print communications project a haphazard, devil-may-care image, that's the way you will be judged—regardless of your actual competence and professionalism. Here are eight ideas to help you present yourself more professionally in print:

1. Strive for consistency

Minimize change. Use the same typeface and color choices throughout all of your print communications. Don't use Times Roman (a popular typeface) for your brochure, Garamond (another popular typeface) on your business card and Arial (yet another typeface design) in your newsletter. Choose a core set of typefaces and a consistent color palette of a limited number of colors that work well together. Faithfully use these throughout all of your print communications.

2. Add white space

Avoid cramped pages. Use white space—the absence of text or graphics—to make your publications project a distinct and easy-to-read image. Use white space in the margins of your publications to focus your reader's eyes on your message as well as make it easy for readers to hold your brochure or newsletter without their thumbs obscuring some of the words.

3. Chunk content

Insert frequent subheads to break long articles into a series of easier-to-read mini-articles. Each subhead advertises the paragraphs that follow and provides an additional entry point into your text.

4. Align elements

Avoid visuals, such as charts, illustrations or photographs that appear seemingly "dropped in" to your pages. Align the borders of your photographs with each other or the underlying column structure that organizes your pages.

5. Exercise restraint

Eliminate unnecessary graphic elements. Today's desktop publishing software makes it too easy to add unnecessary page borders, vertical lines between columns or decorative clipart. Instead, try to make as few "marks" on the page as possible. Just as your writing gains strength by eliminating unnecessary words, your correspondence, brochures and newsletters will project a more professional image, if there is a good reason for every graphic element on the page.

6. Use upper-case type with restraint

Headlines and subheads set entirely in upper case type (i.e., all capital letters) occupy more space and are significantly harder to read than headlines and subheads set in lower case type.

7. Never underline

Underlining instantly projects an amateurish, typewriter-like image. Underlined words are significantly harder to read than the same words set in bold or italics. The only time underlined words should appear in your print publications is to indicate web site addresses and e-mail addresses.

8. Sweat the details

Avoid visual distractions, such as awkward sentence spacing when two spaces are inserted after periods. Avoid widows and orphans--subheads or single lines of text beginning new paragraphs isolated at the bottom of a page or sentence fragments isolated by themselves, at the top of a column or page. Make sure that your software has inserted the proper punctuation, such as curved open and closed quotation marks and apostrophes, rather than straight up-and-down foot and inch marks.

ATTENTION TO DETAIL

Successful Guerrilla Entrepreneurs recognize that their message is judged as much by its appearance as by its content. Don't reserve these tips for formal publications, like brochures and newsletters, printed in color in large numbers by commercial printers. Your everyday correspondence, especially your proposals and reports, deserve as much attention to presentation detail as your formal, printed brochures and newsletters.

[Note: For biographical details on the authors, please refer to p.30.]

CHAPTER 10

THE FOLLOWUP FORMULA

BY GREG ROLLETT

You've heard it before - the fortune is in the followup. There's a good chance that you even believe it. But chances are, you haven't set up a system to actually do the things you know you should be doing to followup with your prospects (or your clients).

Heck, 44% of businesses and sales people give up after one followup. The Marketing Donut recently did a survey that showed that 80% of sales required five followup phone calls after an appointment.

Read that again – **after an appointment.**

How many times do you need to reach out to someone just to get the appointment?

Let me show you how important this can be for your business. Assume you are a dentist. I want you to also assume that your average first year patient value is $4,000. Replace 'dentist' with real estate agent, financial advisor or consultant, if you like.

Every month in your dental practice you receive 100 new leads. These are people that came to your website or saw one of your postcards or were given your information from another patient in your practice. You spent money, time and resources to get them to take that first step.

- How many of them actually booked an appointment?
- How many then showed up to that appointment?
- How many were converted into a client or customer?

Let's do some simple math. I like to keep things simple. For every 100 leads you get into your office, let's say 10 become clients or customers. At $4,000 per customer, that's $40,000 per month.

What happens when you take that same number of leads, and double the number of conversions? That means you don't spend any more money on marketing or ads or direct mail to make the phone ring, but you do focus on adding more value to the 100 people that did want information from you.

From a dollar perspective, doubling the conversions will double your revenue. Heck, for most businesses, closing just 1-2 more new clients every month would mean the world to them.

Let me show you how to do it.

THE FOLLOWUP FORMULA

First, let me tell you that this works for any type of business. I've helped to build this type of system for real estate agents and financial advisors, plus coaches, barber shops and CrossFit gyms.

Ready to get started?

The first step is ensuring that you are properly collecting new leads when they call your office or fill out a form on your website. Here's the truth: if you only collect an email address, you can only email that person. If someone calls your office and all you have is a phone number, you can only call that person.

The most effective followup campaigns incorporate three types of marketing:

1. Email - It's cost effective and you can send them immediately. Plus, you can track everything and know if they opened the email, clicked on a link or completely ignored you.

2. Phone - Yes, you can still call people, talk to them on the phone and do business with folks. In fact, it's generally more effective than email as you can learn and adapt live on the call.

3. Mail - My favorite place to play. No one else does it (or does it well) so you will be playing on a field of one, which gives you a huge competitive advantage.

Now, when every lead calls your office or goes to your landing page or website, you need to do everything in your power to get all three of these ways to followup.

If you lose one, you lose 33% of your followup power. If you lose two of them, you lose 67% of your followup power. I want everyone of you at 100%. This is the difference between a business that is crushing it and helping the most people, and a business just getting by. The one crushing it is the one best at the fundamentals, like collecting information on leads. Don't be lazy and don't let your employees be lazy. Laziness is akin to theft - theft of your profits!

Ok, so we have the information, now it's time to deploy the followup campaign.

Let's break it down.

YOUR EMAIL PLAN OF ATTACK

I like to create a 5-step email campaign that is deployed immediately after someone requests more information from you

- whether that request came over the phone or online.

The key to email is speed. InsideSales.com reports that if you send a followup email within 5 minutes, you are 9 times more likely to convert them.

Each of the emails below are sent in consecutive days. Strike while the fire it hot.

The first email is all about value. How you can help someone who has a specific problem that you solve? If someone is calling the dentist, why are they calling? How can you help them alleviate their pain? What value can you provide to them?

I like to do this through video. In the video I use a formula call P.A.S., which is an old copywriting term for Problem, Agitate, Solution.

In the video, I introduce myself and quickly turn the attention to the viewer and address their problem. I talk about them as if I know exactly what it is they are going through. Then I quickly agitate that problem. I talk about the things they can no longer do because of the pain they are in, or the missed opportunities that are costing them money because they don't have the solution. Finally, I introduce myself as the solution and tell them the next steps to working with me.

Don't overcomplicate things. Film it with your iPhone if you have to. And if you don't like filming videos, write a special report or blog post and send people to read it. Don't like writing, record an audio and give them an MP3. Do what comes most natural to you.

Now, in the second email I like to make a reference to the item of value I sent in the first email, but this time I ask them to take action and start moving forward. I like adding value, but the best way I can add value is if we get to work together. This is true for what you do as well.

In the third email I introduce them to someone I have worked with. Here is the subject line . . .

"NAME meet NAME"

The second NAME is the name of someone that has given you a testimonial that helps to drive home how great your services are. At the end of the email you say, "if you want to be like NAME, here's what you need to do to get started today." Then go into your pitch.

In the fourth email you can either introduce them to another client, or introduce them to another resource - maybe another video, a clip from your interview on The Brian Tracy Show or even a PDF copy of your Best-Selling book.

Finally, in email #5, you send them Dean Jackson's famous 9-word email. It goes like this:

Subject: Hey [NAME]

Are you still interested in...

Your Signature

Insert your area of expertise after "are you still interested in" and that's it. So your email might look like this;

"Are you still interested in planning for your retirement?"
"Are you still interested in selling your home?"
"Are you still interested in getting a whiter smile?"

That's it. Let them reply. It's almost magical what happens when you send this email.

YOUR PHONE STRATEGY

So you've mastered email. Now it's time to get on the phone with your prospects. In this followup formula, the phone is used to get their attention or to get them to pay attention.

I like to use the first outbound call to see if they had an opportunity to go through the thing of value I sent through email #1 in the series above. The call goes something like this:

"Hey [name], just seeing if you had an opportunity to check out the [thing of value] that I emailed over to you. Did you get a chance to watch it/read it?"

Then, let them talk. If they did watch it, ask some questions. What did you like about it? What questions did you have? Is that something you'd like to see done in your business?

If they didn't watch it, mention that you'll send it again. Then strike up a conversation. Ask them questions. Learn about them and their needs.

It's very simple.

You can repeat the phone calls as many times as you'd like or have the manpower to control. I like at least a 3-point contact strategy, but sometimes we will call forever.

THE MICRO SHOCK-AND-AWE PACKAGE

If you've made it this far, you are a rock star. Now it's time to turn up the heat a little more. You might have heard me talk at length about a Shock-and-Awe Package - the big box 'o' stuff that shows up at your doorstep that blows people away and makes them want to do business with you.

Today I am going to share a micro shock and awe strategy. You see, not every prospect is created equally. When you are just starting the relationship, you might not want to send the whole burrito when chips and salsa will do. I love burritos by the one. Great way to bribe me or get my attention.

In the Micro Shock-and-Awe, we are simply trying to get someone's attention in the mail box so we have a shot at getting them on the phone or in the office. We are not trying to make the big sale - just the first step.

I like sending the Micro Shock-And-Awe package in a Priority Mail envelope or UPS/FedEx envelope with a cover letter, CD or DVD and a sales letter full of social proof that gets the prospect to take the next step.

That's it. Again, you don't need to overcomplicate things. The best baseball players in the world have the most sound fundamentals - they catch the ball, make accurate throws and can lay down a bunt to move the runner over. This allows them to win games.

The followup system I've shown to you here will help you win games. You might not win the MVP Award and get on the cover of Sports Illustrated, but you'll be laughing all the way to the bank. What's more guerrilla than that?

About Greg

Greg Rollett, @gregrollett, is a Best-Selling Author and Marketing Expert who works with experts, authors and entrepreneurs all over the world. He utilizes the power of new media, direct response and personality-driven marketing to attract more clients and to create more freedom in the businesses and lives of his clients.

After creating a successful string of his own educational products and businesses, Greg began helping others in the production and marketing of their own products and services. He now helps his clients through two distinct companies, Celebrity Expert Marketing and the ProductPros.

Greg has written for *Mashable, Fast Company, Inc.com, The Huffington Post, AOL, AMEX's Open Forum* and others, and continues to share his message helping experts and entrepreneurs grow their business through marketing.

Greg's client list includes Michael Gerber, Brian Tracy, Tom Hopkins, Coca-Cola, Miller Lite and Warner Brothers, along with thousands of entrepreneurs and small-business owners across the world. Greg's work has been featured on FOX News, ABC, NBC, CBS, CNN, *USA Today, Inc. Magazine, The Wall Street Journal, The Daily Buzz* and more.

Greg loves to challenge the current business environment that constrains people to working 12-hour days during the best portions of their lives. By teaching them to leverage marketing and the power of information, Greg loves to help others create freedom in their businesses that allow them to generate income, make the world a better place, and live a radically-ambitious lifestyle in the process.

A former touring musician, Greg is highly sought after as a speaker, who has spoken all over the world on the subjects of marketing and business building.

If you would like to learn more about Greg and how he can help your business, please contact him directly at: greg@dnagency.com or by calling his office at 877.897.4611.

CHAPTER 11

EMOTIONAL CONTENT
– COULD THIS BE THE MISSING KEY TO BRAND LOYALTY?

BY STEVE REICH

I'll admit it. I am an emotional man. When challenged about expressing my emotions, I try to brush it off with excuses of manliness with statements like: "I am not crying, my eyes are just sweating." On one instance, as we left a theater after experiencing a great sports-themed movie, my son said to me, "Dad that's just embarrassing. You didn't just have tears running down your face, but you actually sobbed loudly at one point."

I am not only emotional about movies or music, but I am also emotional about my favorite products.

ACHIEVING DEEP CONNECTION REQUIRES TOUCHING HUMAN EMOTIONS

What influences consumers to be loyal to leading brands?
Is it rational analysis or emotions based?

Top Brand	Emotional Based Reasons	Rational or Analytical Reason
Nike - Just Do It	Primary	Secondary
Harley Davidson	Primary	Secondary
Facebook	Primary	Secondary
Disney	Primary	Secondary

Even top brands, that have strong analytical practical primary reasons to purchase, have focused special efforts on emotional connections to draw stronger loyalty.

Top Brand	Primary and Secondary Reasons People Purchase
Apple	• An attitude of superior creativity • Very high build quality • Premium materials and components • Great customer service when an error does arise

GUERRILLA MARKETING INSISTS THAT WE UNDERSTAND THE EMOTIONAL CONNECTION BETWEEN OUR CLIENTS AND THE PRODUCTS OR SERVICES WE OFFER

Making a connection:
A connection implies both parties giving input.
- By giving your prospective customer opportunities to give input, they become more invested and loyalty builds quicker.
- Be brave enough with your content to allow for input, opinions, suggestions and content.

Some companies worry that this gives people a public venue to air negative comments . . . it might. However, if your product or service is honest and sound (most of the time), you will not have to defend your product. Your loyal customers will do it for you. Loyal consumers defending your product is much more valuable,

believable and long lasting than anything you could say.
Often marketing efforts are focused on selling a price point or a
single feature. This is a short-term viewpoint and does not take
in the possibility of reaping many purchases over a lifetime.

This chapter focuses on the relationship *between resonating
shared emotions and increased profitability.*

CAN EMOTIONAL CONNECTIONS SAVE MARKETING DOLLARS?

Hypothesis: If consumers buy your product or service because
of likability, loyalty or being emotionally invested, then the cost
of obtaining new customers and keeping customers should be
reduced.

OUR DESIRED RESULTS:
Lower marketing, advertising, P.R., and promotional costs.

- Your message is more memorable, so less frequency is
  needed.
- Emotional investment causes deeper interest so your message
  is shared more between peers, family and friends. – So, less
  purchased media is needed (reach).
- People are purchasing your product because of other reasons
  beyond "lowest price." So your promotional spend doesn't
  have to be as deep (less loss-leaders).

RESONATING SHARED EMOTIONS = INCREASED PROFITABILITY

A direct and measurable benefit can be found by addressing
today's consumer in an emotional manner.

CHANGE YOUR COMMUNICATION TO BUILD THE EMOTIONAL CONNECTION

1. Tell a story.

The greatest teacher ever was known to connect through telling a story. Tell your company's story. Not just your differentiating points but express your passions and excitement.

> 1. Make them feel important. Their support is desired.
>
> **Birth of Likability**

> 2. Promote differentiating qualities that solve consumer's problems.
>
> Adoption

2. Recognize the needs or wants that are being satisfied.

Each product or service purchased helps provide a deeper solution.

Potato Chips – solving the deeper need
a) Chips are good tasting snacks and are priced right.
b) Chips are the seeds for a huge gathering of family and friends. Chips connect people. Chips make you popular. Chips bring fun to a busy life. If you want to have a fun party – you have to have chips!

3. Who are the Heroes?

Marketing often focuses on helping to solve our consumers' problems. However, what if the hero of your story was the consumer? (People love to accept credit for finding a great product or company.) GIVE THEM OPPORTUNITIES to brag about and defend your product or service through social content, etc.

> 3. Provide opportunities for consumers to defend your product or service.
>
> Defender

> *Defending a service or product creates stronger kinship, devotion and loyalty.*

4. Never Stop Caring

Family takes care of family. Strive to continue to deliver every day.

> 4. Family members always are promoters and endorsers.
>
> Family

THE LAW OF FREQUENCY

Frequency is defined as the average number of times an individual notices an advertising message during a defined period of time.

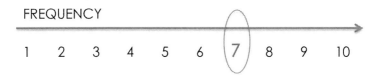

Large companies have calculated the number of times a person needs to see their ads before getting a response. Some companies have determined this number to average around seven times.
– Many large companies calculate their media spend by figuring the cost to get a high percentage of the population to see their message seven times.

A Guerrilla marketer looks at this and says "Seven Times?"

– Why spend that much money when you can improve results benefiting from less frequency by resonating or creating an emotional connection with the target consumers?

If you can get consumer reaction with less media frequency, you save money.

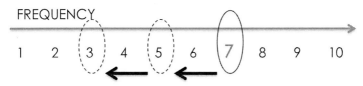

What if you were able to establish an emotional connection that made your message more memorable and likability was established sooner? Could you change the frequency (or number of times a person needs to see your message before acting) to half the established average number? If people are acting on your message after only seeing your ads three to four times, think of the money saved.

RESONATE WITH YOUR DESIRED CONSUMERS

Resonating with your target consumers through touching on the emotions they are experiencing can result in the following:
- Early Adoption
- Likability
- Long-lasting connections – Loyalty
- Increased Profits

Answer truthfully. Have you ever had your mood changed by a song on the radio or a TV commercial? Most of us are scared to admit that emotions are involved in making our decisions. Subconsciously, we want to feel that only logic was involved in our decision-making. Rational analysis of available options is felt as the safe and smart method.

The great Tony Robbins teaches:
PEOPLE BUY FEELINGS, NOT THINGS!

In his great book, *Descartes Error,* Antonio Damasio, professor of neuroscience at the University of Southern California, argues that emotion is a necessary ingredient to almost all decisions.

"When we are confronted with a decision, emotions from previous, related experiences affix values to the options we are considering. These emotions create preferences, which lead to our decisions."

THE PATH TO FAMILY-LIKE LOYALTY

1. Plant the seed of emotional connection . . .
   Then let it grow.
2. Give them a reason to ADOPT . . .
   Then let it grow.
3. Provide an opportunity for them to DEFEND your brand . . .
   Then let it grow.
4. Take care of them like FAMILY

SMART GUERRILLA MARKETERS LOOK TO ADD PASSION, FEELINGS AND HEART-FELT EMOTIONS TO THEIR MARKETING

I hate to admit it, but there was a time when the argument over colas caused a huge rift in a close friendship. My love of a branded cola caused me to raise my emotions to anger as we debated the differences between these products.

- What caused my high emotions?
- What caused my loyalty to a soda pop?

> *A loyalty that was felt as strong as loyalty to my high school, college sports teams or even family.*

As I looked back trying to identify the birth of my allegiance to this brand, I was surprised at how uneventful this all started. During high school I worked as a department manager in a grocery store. In the store, the competing soda pop companies would keep extra inventory in the back room because of the high velocity of product sales. Each company had a determined area to keep their extra inventory product confined. One of the companies did an incredible job of keeping their inventory stacked perfectly straight. No clutter. Their products were easy to access to refill shelves. The other company . . . seemed as if they didn't care.

> 1. Cared about making my Job run smoother –
>
> Birth of Likability

> 2. Encourage adaptability by making me feel like a member of their brand.
>
> Adoption

As a department manager it was my responsibility to make sure the store was clean, full and easy to shop. Because of the efforts of this one company being focused on making my job easier, I began to be a fan of their products. I felt their company understood me, respected me and sincerely wanted to help me.

> 3. Usage grew and support increased as I was put into a position to defend the brand.
>
> **Defender**

This company, in addition to doing a great job, also pulled me into their brand by providing me with research, educating me on current trends, etc. They made me feel important. They made me feel part of their brand including a logoed golf-shirt or a logoed pen. Eventually my support was strong enough that I would proudly scoff at a waiter if a particular restaurant didn't have my favorite pop on tap. I was occasionally pulled into discussions of which brand was better, and so I pridefully defended this brand.

> 4. Celebrate successes and victories.
> **Protector of the Brand**
>
> **Family**

Again: This is not a touching emotional story. However, because seeds of an emotional connection were planted within me (LIKABILITY), I started to become a fan. My likability for the brand was enhanced with every advertisement or sponsorship. With the seed planted, their Marketing, P.R. and promotional efforts fueled my likability to later develop into incredible FAMILY-LIKE LOYALTY.

THE PATH TO FAMILY-LIKE LOYALTY

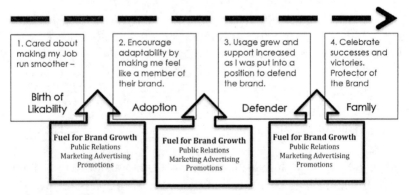

Birth of Likability
- Can be an emotional connection or a strong rational analysis.

Adoption
- Adds Emotional Connection to a previous Rational Analysis – or Adds Rational Analysis to a previous Emotional Connection.

Defender
- A situation in which the adopter needs to act as defender of the brand – increases the level of support the individual has for the brand.

Family
- Brands that make it to this level enjoy proactive support and protection of the brand by loyal users.

EMOTIONAL MARKETING MUST ALSO INCLUDE THE CONNECTION

NOTE: Just being FUNNY, SEXY, TOUGH, CARING OR COMPASSIONATE in your advertising is not enough.

Have you heard a conversation like this?
- Remember that great Super Bowl ad from last year? The one that had us laughing so hard your brother blew chip dip out his nose?
- Yeah – that was great. What was the ad for?
- I don't remember, but it sure was funny.

These ads failed! - They forgot their job was to make the emotional connection between their product or service and the consumer. Although they provided emotion, the connection between the product and the emotion was not made.

Do not throw away money on just hitting any emotion. Focus on the emotion behind the solution your product brings to the consumer.

WHAT EMOTIONAL FEELINGS INFLUENCE US?

Self Confidence
- We want to look better.
- We want to be thinner or taller.
- We want to be in control.
- We want to feel love and happiness.
- We want to feel desired.

More Control
- We want to save money.
- We want to save time.
- We want to feel safe.
- We want to be worry-free.

Self–Worth - Desire to Contribute
- We want to be good at our role in our family.
- We want to be appreciated in our role in our occupation.
- We want to be recognized for our accomplishments and good decisions.

Charles Revson of the great Revlon cosmetics company said:

In the factory we make cosmetics,
In the store we sell hope!

Having the same attitude that Charles Revson expressed we can identify the emotional traits that we can deliver.

Example:

Product	Possible Emotions
Cosmetics	- Hope, Self-Worth
New Car	- Self Confidence, Safety
Cup Cakes	- Comfort, Well-being

Various industries execute their emotional marketing in different manners. Recently working with companies that promote counseling and therapy, we found that if a potential customer **could see the emotions and passions** of the counselors or therapists, they were much more willing to call the company to discuss possible help.

Here is an example of our thought process:

- For this client, our thinking went as follows:
    - It's harder to feel emotions or passions from a print advertisement. – Let's look at media that can best

show the emotions and passions we feel for our cause: Video, TV, Maybe Radio

- ◆ TV commercials generally limited to 60, 30 or 15 seconds don't leave us enough time to share our emotional story. – Options: Social Media, videos, TV appearances, segments on local news or talk shows.

We ended up booking time on Midday News (approx. 4 minute segments) and in both morning and afternoon local TV talk formats.

Here's how we benefitted:
1. Viewers were able to see the emotions of the counselors: **Real People**
2. Attached faces to the company: **Increased Trust**
3. 3rd party endorsement: Perception - our company was doing such great things that the TV stations took notice and wanted to report it. **Credibility**

MEASURED RESULTS:

Client: Counseling and Therapy
Number of Clients: 22 – beginning efforts
Number of Clients: 165 – 4 ½ months later

The key to emotional connection was the pre and post efforts in social media with the TV segments.

Condensed Example: -

Social Media Plan:

- • **Leading up to the day of the TV segment:**
  - ◆ 1 week prior - posted on the company's website and

social media sites that we have the opportunity to be on TV to tell our story.

- ◆ All employees of the company were encouraged to share this with family and friends that they thought would benefit.

- **The Day the segment airs:**
  - ◆ Big Build up that morning – (Today is the day! Watch for us on TV at 12:10 on the midday news.)
  - ◆ Potential future clients that had shown some interest were emailed inviting them to watch.

- **Days after the segment airs:**
  - ◆ Posted "As seen on TV" a clip of the segment on all social media and websites.
  - ◆ The TV station archives these segments on their website for 1 year. We made sure the segment had links to our website. We made sure our website also had the segment linking to the TV station.
  - ◆ Future brochures, print ads, etc., included: As seen on KZTV15.
  - ◆ Framed photo in the lobby of the counselor on TV.

By embracing the emotional points surrounding this business we were able to leap frog over competition and reach financial success sooner.

> *They may forget what you said — but they will never forget how you made them feel.*
> ~ Carl W. Buehner

Emotional Connection – **Beats** – Price
P.R. and Social Media – **Out Lasts** – Promotion

RISE ABOVE THE CLUTTER!

Connecting with your target consumer is more difficult today than ever before. When you view the statistics comparing the volume of ads and impressions the average person wades through daily, you see the difficulty.

However, the opportunities to develop consumers into: ADAPTORS, DEFENDERS AND FAMILY are more prevalent with today's social communities than ever before.

Grab the attention of the consumer by being interesting, creative and connecting with their lifestyles. Add the passions and emotions you feel to your P.R., Marketing, Promotions and especially your Social Content. Connect with your target consumers by showing you understand what they are feeling.

Create the emotional consumer connection.

About Steve

Steve Reich is an American entrepreneur, marketer and public speaker who specializes in guerrilla style marketing, launching new products and promoting the buy local effort. Reich was Vice President of Marketing of a $2 billion company for over 20 years, focused on growth of over 500 retail stores of all sizes in the Western United States. His love of non-traditional marketing trends and measured promotional efforts shows through in his passionate drive.

Currently Steve is president and CEO of R Marketing. He is devoted to helping entrepreneurs to market their efforts in new and exciting ways. He is an avid supporter of the Buy Local movement and donates much of his time to helping local businesses succeed.

Although Reich works with businesses all over the world, he currently resides in Syracuse, Utah. Reich welcomes conversations, idea sharing and marketing connections.

CHAPTER 12

SEVEN PILLARS OF PROSPERITY
– THE BEGINNING

BY DR. DOUG GULBRANDSEN

My father, Norman Gulbrandsen, passed away in 2010 at the age of 92 years. He had lived a long and productive life. He had developed a national reputation as one of the leading university-level classical voice teachers during his time at Northwestern University and DePaul University.

As our family prepared for his funeral, we received an interesting request. A couple of his past students, now professors of music at Northwestern University, asked if we would be ok if they planned a memorial concert on his behalf at the University. We thought it would be a wonderful way to pay honor to his life and contribution to his students, so we were more than willing.

As it turned out, they had some leading classical singers (who had been his students) fly in from all over the country to participate. It was a wonderful program, with musical solos from them, interspersed with stories from others of his students who had been asked to share their thoughts. It was engaging, emotional, and oftentimes a bit humorous as they told the personal stories about their interaction with my dad.

One specific story really touched me. One of his students shared how he had become good friends with my dad, although there was a significant age difference. They used to play tennis together often, (even though dad should have stopped playing tennis a few years prior because of his advancing age). As he shared the stories of some of their tennis matches, most of which were very humorous, he said that once in a while, dad would honestly and fairly beat him. And he wondered, how on earth…? And then he gave the answer, "Norman had **willed** me off the court."

He then shared another story of when he flew to Germany to audition for a national opera. He was in competition with the national favorite tenor for the part. He shared how hard he practiced the night before the audition, and when the audition was over, not only was he awarded the specific opera, but was also awarded the opportunity to be the lead tenor for the entire season. As he walked off the stage in utter bewilderment, he asked himself, how…? And then it came to him. He had **willed** his competition off the stage. And he recognized the impact dad had had in his life.

I had no idea of the impact this experience would have on my life. My life and direction changed at this moment in time. As I walked out of the concert, I gathered together with my four brothers and sister and made this comment: "Do you realize the impact that dad had on his students?" Because there was a common message that was communicated by each of his students that participated, "Yes, Norman taught us how to sing (well), but maybe more importantly, he gave us the will to win, to succeed, to live, and to love."

I asked myself, how can I affect the greatest changes for good in another person's life? Over the years I had observed that implementing correct business principles filtered over into personal lives in almost a one-to-one fashion.

And my personal journey began: to positively affect as many

lives as I could through the use of my talents, which was to help business owners through executive coaching and operational and management consulting, to become profitable in their businesses, and prosperous in their lives.

Let me share an example. Onc of the basic keys to a profitable and prosperous business is to understand the purpose (or the driving force) behind the company. What is the effect (or impact) that your product or service will have on the people who purchase from you? Is part of your purpose to truly serve your clients or customers; to give them a "wow" experience? Consider how this concept applies in your personal life. Your friends, your special relationships, do you focus on helping them to have a "wow" experience with your interaction with them? Are you acknowledging them with thank you cards, or at least a verbal thank you? Are you listening to them with a desire to truly understand their communication? So, here is the question, am I talking about business or personal? It's hard to distinguish, isn't it?

So I determined that I could best serve others by serving them in their business. Because when finances or lack of time becomes a problem in their business, the personal side of a business owner's life usually becomes an issue.

In my quest to most effectively help business owners to experience profitability and a life of prosperity, I have assimilated the best of the best business principles and practices that I have learned along the way, and developed a proven process to prosperity, which I call the *Seven Pillars of Prosperity*.

I think it is important to distinguish between profitability and prosperity.

Prosperity:
1. A state of health, happiness, and prospering.
2. Steady good fortune or financial security.

Profitability:
1. The quality of affording gain or benefit or profit.
2. Gainfulness, lucrativeness, profitableness

You can have anything you want if you want it badly enough. You can be anything you want to be, do anything you set out to accomplish, if you hold to that desire with singleness of purpose.
~ Abraham Lincoln

This statement has been the basis of the Be-Do-Have paradigm. It is an inspired statement for all people, and especially for the business owner. The challenge is to understand the sequence that leads to prosperity, and personal fulfillment.

As I've begun working with clients, I have observed an interesting phenomenon (and I have to admit, in full disclosure, that I was guilty to some degree also at one point in my life) of those who mixed the sequence up. You might have observed the same thing in your area. They purchased a big home, nice car, and expensive clothes (have) to appear successful (be). The challenge becomes making enough money to pay for it all on a monthly basis (do). When the economy changes downward, the personal stress moves upward exponentially.

The correct order is Be-Do-Have. The key to what Abraham Lincoln said is the "singleness of purpose." When you establish your purpose first, and make sure that the "Do" and "Have" align with that purpose, you are on your path to prosperity.
In this chapter, I focus on the first, and foundational step, BE. So let's get started.

BE

This is the foundation of your success and prosperity. It includes two different sections: a) who you are, and b) what your business represents, and the legal and financial protection for your company and family.

Under section a) you will find Your Personal Purpose, Your Personal Constitution, Your Integrity, Your Leadership Qualities, and a Clear Path.

YOUR PERSONAL PURPOSE

I recall working with a client in Sacramento, California. He was making all sorts of unwise (and costly) business decisions. As I sought to understand the basis for this, I finally called him and told him we needed to have a "soul searching" session. We got together and spent the next two hours exploring in depth what was really important to him. In the end we discovered that where he was in his personal and business life was a far distance from where his true purposes would have placed him. There existed this tremendous gap between where he was, and where he wanted to be. And that subconscious stress was causing bad decisions. Once he regrouped and got aligned with his inner purpose, he was off and running successfully toward that life of prosperity.

In *The 7 Habits of Highly Effective People,* by Steven R. Covey, Habit #2 is "Begin with the End in Mind." As my friend, Dan Clark (contributing author to the *Chicken Soup for the Soul* series) mentioned during a discussion we had, there is a missing ingredient that needs to be mentioned, and that is firstly establishing your true purpose. It is essential that you take the time to really discover what is important to you at the deepest level. What is your purpose in life? How does it transcend you from a taker to a true server of others? How does your life purpose translate into your business purpose? There are different exercises you can go through that will help you do this. The key is to use this as a foundation for everything else you do. If you keep this always in mind, and base your decisions for a specific direction in your business, you will stay on the right path. Once you have established your purpose, then looking forward to what the ideal scene for you and your business becomes the next logical step, but now it has the correct foundation.

Later on in his life, Maslow added an additional step to his hierarchy of needs, and that was "Self-transcendence." "This may involve service to others, devotion to an ideal (e.g., truth, art) or a cause (e.g., social justice, environmentalism, the pursuit of science, a religious faith), and/or a desire to be united with what is perceived as transcendent or divine." Have you done sufficient introspection to understand the importance of that level in your life's purpose? I can tell you unequivocally, that it is never about the money. There are too many millionaires and billionaires out there who are not happy that prove that statement. As many business leaders and consultants are now learning, it is all about purpose and impact. The money naturally follows.

YOUR VALUES

What are your personal values? There are many exercises available to help you determine what your most basic values are. Sometimes it will surprise you what lies at the depths of your heart.

There is one such exercise that I learned from my personal coach, Sean Smith. He has given me permission to share it with you. If you go to: **http://prosperityvalues.com**, you can download the exercise. It is self-explanatory. You will need a partner to effectively do the exercise. Have your spouse or a good friend team up with you and follow the instructions to a tee. You may be surprised at the results, but it will become the basis for everything you do.

YOUR PERSONAL CONSTITUTION

Have you considered writing a "Personal Constitution" that will include those personal values? Much like the U.S. Constitution, it can be the foundation for all of your decision making? I encourage you to do it.

YOUR INTEGRITY

Your Integrity will be the measure of how well you stick to your Personal Constitution in your business and personal decisions. How often have you met someone whom you felt you could trust, and then got taken advantage of? How did you feel about that person? Don't you be the one who says one thing and does another. Let both your word and your actions stay aligned and true.

Have you ever heard the words, "personal is personal, and business is business?" In my mind, that is just an excuse for a lack of personal and business integrity. Your business must represent the same high values that you have established as an individual. When people recognize your company for high values and integrity, your customer and client base growth will be unstoppable.

YOUR LEADERSHIP QUALITIES

Your Leadership Qualities will be reflected in how you lead, treat and train others according to your Personal Constitution. Each area combined determines who you are and how you will genuinely represent yourself to clients/customers, your employees, and your friends and family.

As you continue on this path, recognize that you become the sum total of those with whom you associate. That not only includes your friends and associates, but just as important, those whom you hire to help you in your business. How much drama do you experience with your business team? If it is a lot, then you need to make some changes. It becomes your responsibility to hire the right people, and then train them in the same leadership qualities that have helped you to become that great individual and leader.

YOUR CLEAR PATH

I remember having a discussion with Hyrum Smith, co-founder

of Franklin-Covey and author of the recent book, *3 Gaps: The Journey to Inner Peace*. He emphasized the point that if we are not ultimately experiencing the outcomes we desire, both in life and in business, it ultimately boils down to our inner belief system, which then dictates our values and actions.

The "clear path" section is really important, because I see many business owners sabotaging their own efforts. They have disempowering, subconscious beliefs and habits that reflect their values and actions, and present insurmountable obstacles in their path. These beliefs and habits must, I repeat, must be handled to move forward. I have personally seen miracles occur with clients and their business when they are willing to address and handle these items.

YOUR BUSINESS, LEGAL AND PERSONAL FINANCIAL PROTECTION

The second foundational aspect is making sure that your business and family are financially and otherwise protected. Have you consulted both an attorney and accountant to make sure you, your business, and your family are protected from a legal standpoint? Have you attended to all the insurance needs that you should have? There is no way to "catch up" when the need suddenly arises. You must play "defense" and protect yourself from the beginning.

Now is the time to make the decision to be prudent in your personal finances and your family involvement.

All too often I see the same pattern when it comes to finance. As you earn more income, the cost of your lifestyle increases. Suddenly you may find yourself robbing Peter to pay Paul. When the economy turns down for a period of time, you may find that your personal expenses don't. Thus you have to maintain a certain withdrawal of money from your company to keep up on a personal level. That has quite an effect on your business capital.

LIVE WITHIN YOUR MEANS

So how do you prevent that from happening? The answer is to live within your means, and truly understand what that number is. Your means is determined by what your business allows you to withdraw on a bi-weekly or monthly basis. That number is not, I repeat, not determined by your gross revenue. Make sure your spouse and children understand what that means.

As you lay the foundation of BE in your business and your life, the other actions of DO and HAVE will naturally follow.

In my book, *The Seven Pillars of Prosperity,* I discuss the necessary action steps for DO and HAVE.

BE Profitable and BE Prosperous!

About Dr. Doug

What sets Dr. Doug Gulbrandsen, a Marketing & Growth Strategist, apart from the typical business process improvement consultant? In one word, ***mentoring.*** Doug's extensive hands-on business consulting business was gleaned from 34-plus years of operating two different types of businesses that he owned, including a dental practice. This equipped Doug with an extensive knowledge base in business process management.

As he observed bright and highly capable dental professionals operating their practices in a less-than-optimal fashion, and other types of businesses doing the same thing, he recognized there is a consistency of what is needed in every type of business. In a few words, it is: *"identifying the gaps between 'best practices' for a specific type of business versus the 'existing practices', and then closing those gaps so that increased efficiency, productivity, and profitability is achieved."*

Subsequently, Doug left his private practice – one that had spanned two decades – choosing to increase his knowledge in business process management by going back to business school. He took those insights he had gleaned from his years of operating his two businesses, and the best practices protocol he learned in business school, to merge together an effective and strategic business model that can be implemented by business owners within their company.

The results are staggering. Any business can be helped to climb up to a new and higher level of profitability, giving the business owner greater control and predictability of his future business through performance key indicators. *Managing by measuring is one of the most effective tools that is in use today by the most successful companies, and now can easily be integrated into the small business model.*

He provides business management solutions to clients on a nationwide basis. Many clients have said utilizing Doug's consultative services is one of the **best investments they have ever made.**

Doug currently resides in Draper, UT, with his wife Linda. He has four amazing children, Michael, Thomas, Phillip and Rachael.

CHAPTER 13

MARKETING YOURSELF AS A SUCCESSFUL GUERRILLA ENTREPRENEUR

BY JAY CONRAD LEVINSON AND JEANNIE LEVINSON

Successful Guerrilla Entrepreneurs know that success involves not only choosing the right Guerrilla Marketing weapons, but also using them as effectively as possible. Appearance plays a major role in the effectiveness of your success. You must always be "on," projecting yourself in as favorable a way as possible.

Graphic design plays a major role in determining the image you project in your marketing materials. From the appearance of your ads, brochures, business cards, newsletters, presentation visuals and web site, prospects will make instant decisions about your credibility and ability to satisfy their needs.

Accordingly, it's vital that you become aware of some of the subtle influences that can promote or hinder the image you project to clients and prospects. After analyzing your current marketing materials, you may want to redo some of them in order to project a fine-tuned and positive image.

This chapter also focuses on the image you project to clients and prospects who meet you face-to-face.

Are you best described as neat and clean or casual? Is it possible to figure out what you had for breakfast yesterday from your shirt? Do you need a haircut? Appearance plays a major role in determining the image you project in print, in person and online.

DESCRIBING YOUR BUSINESS TO YOUR PROSPECTS

You can have the best product or service in the world, but many potential clients won't be interested in your professional services unless you can convince them in a very personal way.

There are two steps you should consider to define your marketing message.

Let's take a short quiz to see how well you accomplish this:

Step 1:
Describe your business in ten seconds or less. In this exercise, use seven words or less:
- Example (1) "We coach businesses to increase their profits."
- Example (2) "We sell computers at the lowest prices."
The goal here is to create focus and to arouse curiosity.

How would you describe your business in seven words or less?

Step 2:
After engaging a person's interest, you can describe your business in more detail, using an interactive conversational style. Be sure to address the benefits of your service and your competitive advantage. Use words that inspire.

PRESENTING YOURSELF

Guerrilla Entrepreneurs realize that their clients and customers judge their competence at every point of contact. Accordingly, successful Guerrilla Entrepreneurs pay constant attention to the way they present themselves and strive for constant improvement. There are two categories of presentations: *time-lapse and realtime.*

1. Time-lapse presentations

Time-lapse presentations are characterized by a delay between the time the successful Guerrilla Entrepreneur prepares his or her message and the time their clients or prospects read it. Their message may be prepared hours, days, weeks, or months ahead of time. As a result, time-lapse presentations are one-way communications: they cannot be changed "on the fly", since they can't observe every reader's reaction.

This delay between creation and reading, places a great burden on the appearance or formatting of the Guerrilla's message. Their entire message must compensate for the facial expressions, gestures and vocal intonations that readers can't see but use to judge messages that are delivered face-to-face. As a result, time-lapse communications are extremely detail intensive.

Formatting errors, such as the random placement of text and graphics on a page, or the inconsistent use of color and type, constantly changing typeface and type size undermines the message. Likewise, editing problems like transposed words or spelling errors destroy the image of competence and professionalism that Guerrilla Entrepreneurs strive to project, at every point of contact.

CATEGORIES

There are three types of time-lapse communications:
i. Print: ads, brochures, business cards, newsletters, proposals and reports.
ii. Online: your website, digital marketing and webinars
iii. E-mail: including e-mail sent to clients as well as postings to online forums.

2. Real-time communications

Real-time presentations are *two-way communications:* Guerrillas not only enhance their message with gestures by varying their tone of voice, but also drive home their point by maintaining eye contact and occasionally smiling.

Guerrillas can alter their real-time presentation by observing their client's reaction to their words. They can read their client's body language and react accordingly.

There are four types of real-time presentations:

 i. *Telephone:* or teleconferencing – efficiently and friendly incoming or outgoing calls are placed and handled.
 ii. *Face-to-face:* One-to-one or group presentations in a conference room or at a speaker's podium.
 iii. *Online*: Such as social media – and how well do you engage your "friends."
 iv. *Live broadcast:* such as Periscope, Meerkat, Blab or Facebook live.

****

"You only have one chance to make a good first impression."

****

YOU ARE ALWAYS ON-STAGE

Whether you know it or not, you're marketing yourself every day. And *to lots of people!* You're marketing yourself to make a sale, warm up a relationship, get a job, get connected, and get something you deserve. You're always sending messages about yourself.

INTENTION

Guerrilla Entrepreneurs control the messages that they send—*it's all about intention!* Non-guerrillas send unintentional messages, even if those messages sabotage their overall goals in life. They want to close a sale for a consulting contract, but their inability to make eye contact or the mumbled message they leave on an answering machine turns off the prospect.

Guerrilla Entrepreneurs send no unintentional messages. Unintentional messages erect an insurmountable barrier. Your job: be sure there is no barrier. There are really two people within you – your accidental self and your intentional self. Most people are able to conduct about 95 percent of their lives by intent. But that's not enough. It's the other 5 percent that can get you in trouble – or in clover.

We're not talking phoniness here. The idea is for you to be who you are and not who you aren't – to be aware of what you're doing, aware of whether or not your actions communicate ideas that will help you get what you deserve.

TAKE A PERSONAL INVENTORY

How do you send messages and market yourself right now?

- Your appearance
- You also market with your eye contact
- Body language
- Your habits
- Your speech patterns
- You market yourself in print with your letters, email, website, notes, faxes, brochures and other printed material
- You market yourself with your attitude
- You also market yourself with your ethics

HOW DO PEOPLE JUDGE YOU?

Again, you may not be aware of it, but people are constantly judging and assessing you by noticing many things about you. You must be sure the messages of your marketing don't fight your dreams.

What are people using to base their opinions, to make their decisions about you?

* Clothing * Hair * Weight * Height * Jewelry * Facial hair * Makeup * Business card * Laugh * Glasses * Title * Neatness * Smell * Teeth * Smile * What you carry * Eye contact * Gait * Posture * Tone of voice * Handwriting * Spelling * Hat * Thoughtfulness * Car * Office * Home * Nervous habits * Handshake * Stationery * Availability * Writing ability * Phone use * Enthusiasm * Energy level * Comfort online

You're fully aware of your intentional marketing and possibly even invest time, energy and imagination into it, not to mention money.

But you may be undermining that investment if you're not paying attention to things that matter to others even more than what you say:

- keeping promises
- punctuality
- honesty
- demeanor
- respect
- gratitude
- sincerity
- feedback
- initiative
- reliability

They also notice passion -- or the absence of it
They notice how well you listen to them.

RELATIONSHIPS FOR SUCCESSFUL GUERRILLA ENTREPRENEURS

No man—and no business—is an island.

Guerrillas strive for and savor long-term relationships with their customers. They well know the myriad of benefits of long-lasting connections and do all in their power to establish and nourish them. They're well aware that *it costs them six times more to sell something to a prospect than to sell that same thing to a customer.*

It's one thing, however, to know the value of a long-term relationship and it's something entirely different to *engage in activities* that spawn such delicious connections.

■Relationship chemistry

The chemistry of a long-term relationship is as complex as the chemistry of a long-term and happy marriage. The starting point is a commitment to the happiness of someone else.

The next point is a goal not of customer satisfaction, because that's relatively simple and common, but of *customer bliss*—exceeding the expectations of customers, *giving more* than they anticipated, *caring more* than they're used to sellers caring.

To do this, you've got to *learn about them.* You learn first by listening to them, then by asking more questions and listening carefully once again. Successful Guerrilla Entrepreneurs often ask those questions on their web site or with specially-prepared customer questionnaires, which solicit personal information.

By knowing the personal likes and dislikes of your customers you can render personalized service—such as clipping articles of interest to special customers or recognizing their achievements and the achievements of their families or businesses.

Here are some additional ways to use a personal touch when dealing with customers:

- ♦ Handwritten notes on mailings make the customers feel singled out.
- ♦ Phone calls that are not part of a telemarketing campaign accomplish the same.
- ♦ Using the customers' names, talking with them of non-business topics, alerting them to special new products or services you have available, responding instantly to their calls and emails, faxes and letters.

■Details

All those seemingly insignificant actions act as beneficial catalysts in the chemistry of a healthy buyer-seller relationship. The more details you know of your customers' lives and businesses, the more empowered you are to mention those details, making each customer feel unique and special rather than part of a large demographic group.

Guerrillas have the insight to know that there's an extraordinary chemistry that exists in long-term relationships. It doesn't happen automatically. It doesn't happen instantly. But when it does happen, the business owner is as delighted as the customer.

■Are you an EFFECTIVE RELATIONSHIP BUILDER?

Read each statement and rate yourself on a scale of from 1 to 10, (with 1 = never, 10 = always). Answer every question not only from your own perspective, but as a client or customer would answer for you.

Taking your "relationship inventory":

1. I strike up conversations with strangers and share my business frequently with them.
2. My marketing plan includes attending regular networking events.
3. I remember personal details about people and share them at an appropriate moment to let them know I care about them.
4. My clients are a great source of referrals, which I tap on a regular basis.
5. I follow-up with potential clients within 48 hours.
6. I believe that everyone is a potential client.
7. When I'm out and about, I look and act professional.
8. I'm fun to be around. People love to talk to me.
9. My community can count on me to be there. I often participate in community programs and frequently volunteer.
10. I feel confident in myself.
11. I remember to acknowledge people's strengths.
12. I enjoy speaking in front of groups.
13. I sell my services to a person, not another client or a corporation.
14. People are extraordinary. I look for the good in all people.
15. My business is oriented to giving. I often provide free consultations, tips, gifts and information.
16. I ask my friends to introduce me to potential clients.
17. People contribute to me on a regular basis.
18. I see myself as a resource for others.
19. My networking and relationship building skills have produced many clients over the last six months.

[Note: For biographical details on the authors, please refer to p.30.]

CHAPTER 14

THE PERSONALITY OF A SUCCESSFUL GUERRILLA ENTREPRENEUR

BY JAY CONRAD LEVINSON AND JEANNIE LEVINSON

It's going to be an uphill battle to become a successful Guerrilla Entrepreneur unless you've got certain personality traits. We're sure that you've already got some, if not most, of these traits already. But you need all of them.

While creating marketing programs for many of the largest, wealthiest and most successful companies on earth, as well as some of the smallest, newest and most poorly funded, we've studied the leaders of those bound for success – in the quest for personality characteristics that they have in common. We've found an even dozen. Those companies on the *Fortune 500* and headed for the *Fortune 500* have had marketing campaigns masterminded by honchos with these twelve traits.

We've looked for exceptions, but have found none. Does that mean that if you have these traits, you'll succeed? It does not. But it does mean that unless you have them, the odds are seriously against you. And that's no way to start any guerrilla marketing venture. By *consciously trying to develop the personality characteristics that you don't have now,* you'll be putting the odds in your favor, a highly-desirable state for any self-respecting guerrilla marketer.

Your goal: to possess all twelve traits. Our goal: to show you how to do that. You probably won't need a personality transplant, but you may need to sharpen some of the rough edges lest they trip you up.

The First Trait: Patience

The determination of this trait began with a study in which researchers were asked a very tough question: "How many times must a person be exposed to your message in order to transform them from total apathy, meaning, they've never heard of you, to purchase readiness, which means they're dying to buy from you?" Astonishingly, the researchers came up with an answer. It was **nine**. *A person must be exposed to your message nine times before they're ready to buy from you.* That's the good news. The bad news is that for every three times you put out the word and expose them to your message, they're only paying attention one time. After all, they do have more important things to do with their lives than focus on your marketing.

So you put out the word three times and your message penetrates their mind one time. What happens then? Nothing happens. So you put out the word six times and penetrate their minds two times. What happens then? They faintly realize that they've heard your name before. But that's as far as it goes. Now you put out the word nine times, penetrating their minds three times. What happens then? Something does happen: they realize they've seen or heard your marketing before, and they know that unsuccessful companies don't market. The momentum has started, but they're not even close to buying what you're selling.

Sticking with the drill, you put out the word – by radio, television, newspaper ads, print ads, email, signs, banners, whatever – a total of twelve times, penetrating their minds four times. What happens then? Not much. They may look around for other signs of your existence, perhaps even ask a friend about you, but they certainly aren't ready to buy from you yet. You put out the word fifteen times, penetrating their minds five times. What happens then? Something wonderful happens. They read every word of your copy. They pay close attention to your commercial. If you list your website – and we sure hope that you do – they click over to it and check you out. If you offer a brochure, they request it. The momentum leading to the sales picks up, but notice – they do not buy from you.

At this point, you begin to feel frustrated. After all, you've peppered your market with powerful messages, but they do not beat a path to your door. It does enter their minds to own what you're selling, but they are just plain not ready to buy from you. Not yet. Maybe never. Here's where most business owners abandon their campaigns. They figure they're doing everything wrong and that they need a new message, new media, a revamped website. The truth is that they're doing everything right. But marketing just doesn't do what they expected it to do. They expected it to work in a hurry.

Listen up. Marketing does a lot of good things, wonderful things. But one thing it rarely does is work in a hurry. Get serious. Don't be like those companies which decide to forsake their marketing investments and start all over again at 'square one.' We wince at the thought. Doing that is called "sellus interruptus." The sale is never consummated. Here's where you've got to hang in there and continue to put out the word. You put it out there eighteen times, penetrating the minds of your increasingly-interested prospects six times. What happens at that point? They begin to think of when they'll make the purchase, where they'll get the money. But they do not buy.

So you put out the word twenty-one times, penetrating their minds seven times. This is when they tell others that they're planning to purchase from you. They may even note it in their datebooks or on their smartphones. Put out the word twenty-four times and you've penetrated their minds eight times. This is when they check with whoever they usually check with before making big ticket purchases. This is when they actually plan the day and the time that they will buy from you. You see nothing to indicate that they're ready to take the plunge onto your customer list. But you continue marketing, putting out the word twenty-seven times. You've penetrated their minds nine times. **Nine times.** What happens then? They come in and they buy from you. They treat you like an old friend. You don't know them from Adam or Eve, but you have built up a strong sense of familiarity and familiarity is the factor that breeds sales.

How on earth did you bring about this blessed state of affairs? You did it with *patience,* the personality trait that opened heavens' doors. Without your patience, it just wouldn't have happened. With patience, it almost always happens. If you don't have patience or can't develop patience, we hope you either leave the marketing department or find another line of work. Patience makes it happen. Some people think that marketing is a miracle-worker. Not true. It's patience that works the miracles.

The Second Trait: Imagination

This trait may not mean what you think it means. It doesn't necessarily mean the creativity to dream up clever headlines, compelling graphics, zippy copy or memorable slogans. Instead, it refers to how you contend with reality.

Lots of companies come up with jazzy headlines, graphics, copy or slogans. If you do too, you're just one in a large crowd. That kind of imagination will not help you stand out in a crowd. What you need is the kind of imagination that helps you stand apart from the crowd. One more clever headline isn't going to do that for you.

In a jam-packed media environment, you need much more than that. You've got to face not only your competition – and we certainly don't want to undermine them because they're getting smarter every day. The real truth is that you've got to face reality head on and you're got to do something to rise above it. You've got to do something your prospects and customers have never seen before so that you can capture and hold their attention better than any competitor anywhere, anytime.

Let's say you're going to do a direct mailing. You certainly won't be the first, but you certainly do want to be the best. How do you do that? By printing something unusual on the envelope? Face it, everybody and their cousin does that. There's no guerrilla genius necessary to come up with a set of words or pictures that will beg the recipient to open their envelope.

But successful Guerrilla Entrepreneurs have the imagination to break through that direct mail clutter and get their mailing noticed, their envelope opened, and their message read. They have the imagination to do something their audience has never seen before and that even you have never seen before.

It begins with their willingness to pop for first-class postage. We're not talking about breaking the bank here. We're only referring to you being willing to invest in 47 cents worth of postage, the cost of a first-class stamp. But you don't buy a 47-cent stamp. Anyone can buy that kind of stamp. You certainly do not use a postage metered stamp because that that has "boring" stamped all over it.

Do you invest in a beautiful, brand new commemorative stamp? Too easy, and to be honest, too common. Instead, you take your 47 cents worth of postage and you invest in fourteen stamps. You buy three six-cent stamps, five three-cent stamps, and seven two-cent stamps. That's fifteen stamps totaling 47 cents, the same as a regular 47-cent stamp.

You put those 15 stamps on the envelopes, do your mailing and realize that when the recipients receive their envelopes, it will probably be the first time in their lives that they've ever seen an envelope with 15 stamps! That envelope will catch their attention first. It will be opened first. And the contents inside will be read first. When you study direct mail, you're taught that the average response rate is 2%. People who send envelopes with 15 stamps enjoy a 20% response rate and even higher. We've heard of response rates surpassing 50%!

Did it take a lot of money? No. But admittedly, it did take a bit more time, a smidgeon more energy, a teeny, tiny more information, and a whale of a better imagination. That's how guerrillas apply their imaginations.

Some, if doing a mailing about a product from England, send their mailings to England so they can be mailing to their prospects with an English stamp. Once again, imagination wins the day for them. With hardly any of your competitors exercising such lively imaginations, it's no surprise that guerrillas win the day through the direct mail. And that's why one of their key personality characteristics is their imagination.

They may not know how to draw their way out of a paper bag or write even two words that rhyme, but when it comes to the imagination to stand apart from reality, they are second to none.

The Third Trait: Sensitivity

A successful Guerrilla Entrepreneur cannot plod through life thinking only of himself or herself. One of the key traits for a truly successful guerrilla is sensitivity.

The Guerrilla Entrepreneurs must be sensitive to:

- the marketplace
- rural or urban environment in which the marketing is taking place

- the economy
- the past history with his products or services, to his customers
- his prospects
- their families
- the time of year
- the competition
- what's on his prospect's minds at the moment he is marketing
- the time in history

****

A lack of this sensitivity was demonstrated in early 2007 during the "Boston Bomb Scare," when a cartoon network owned by Turner Broadcasting promoted – or rather mis-promoted a new TV show by placing decals in all the wrong places: near subways, bus stops, other locales where large groups of people congregated. The decals, which had wires and duct tape attached to them frightened many Bostonians who thought they might be bomb-related. Because two of the jet planes involved in the attack on the World Trade Center in New York in September of 2001 took off from Logan Airport in Boston, it's not hard to blame those citizens of Boston from being terrified, causing traffic and public transportation throughout the city to come to a halt for hours and hours.

Had the promoters been sensitive to the mindset in Boston since 9/11, they could have chosen a different kind of promotion.

Today, there is a pre-9/11 mindset and a post-9/11 mindset, calling for enhanced sensitivity, something the cartoon network promoting totally lacked. That's probably the main reason why the Turner Broadcasting Company was fined $2 million for their insensitivity.

You may not make such a horrific blunder or be fined such a substantial amount, but you could lose a lot of potential profits if you are insensitive. Guerrillas are always sensitive to the code of ethics where they operate, to the sensibilities of the populace, being ultra-careful never to offend people or communities, never to terrify them, never to deface property, never to be intrusive beyond the bounds of good taste.

****

They are sensitive to what their prospects are thinking right at the moment, to what they want, what they lack, what they read about in the newspapers or hear on the radio. They are sensitive to the dreams of their market, striving to make these dreams come true.

As part of mass communication, marketing is part of evolution and has an obligation to be sensitive to everyone, good or bad. Without it, non-guerrillas are fighting an uphill battle.

The Fourth Trait: Ego Strength

By *ego strength,* we don't mean having the ego to stand up to those who don't love you. It's just the opposite, it *means having the ego to stand up to those who love you the most – but give you the worst marketing advice.*

You craft a powerful marketing strategy, embark upon a bound-for-glory campaign, see that all your plans are falling right into place, just as you wanted them to, and who are the first people to tire of your marketing and counsel you to change it? Usually, first it's your co-workers, then your employees, followed closely by your family and then your best friends.
"Hey, you've been doing that marketing for a long time now. I, personally, am getting pretty bored with it. Don't you think it's time to change it?" Your job: Summon up the ego to give these people a nice, warm hug, then send them on their way, knowing they know beans about your marketing.
Those people who have had their minds penetrated by your marketing three times, they're not getting bored with it. They're just learning of your existence. Those folks who have had their minds penetrated five times, the marketing momentum is just

beginning with them. They last thing they want is for you to fade from view. Your current customers, they feel wonderful whenever they're exposed to your marketing because it proves that they've hitched their wagons to a winner – the kind of company that has the confidence to continue to market.

But your co-workers, family and friends, having concentrated on your marketing from the onset, they are tired of it, know it backwards and forwards, wonder when you're going to change it. Again, they not-so-gently hint to you that perhaps you ought to drop it and move on to something else, which is another way of suggesting that you move away from your investment and move away from profitability, move away from the momentum you've established.

It takes a strong ego to look these people in the eye, give their arms a comforting squeeze, then stay with what you started. A lesser person than you, with a weaker ego, might cave in to their pressure, take their well-intended put poorly-reasoned advice, and throw a marketing investment to the winds where, alas, many marketing investments end up.

If you ever thought that guerrilla marketing, especially at the beginning, is a cup of tea, this is the point where you learn that it's not for amateurs, not for insecure babies, and more like a cup of nitroglycerine which can blow up in your face if you make a crucial mistake. Lacking the ego to stand up to misinformed well-wishers is that mistake. If you're a guerrilla, you won't make it. For if you do, you're destined to repeat it each time you're at the helm of a failing business.

The Fifth Trait: Aggressiveness

When you hear that there 200 guerrilla marketing weapons and that more than half of them are free, if you're a Guerrilla Entrepreneur, a smile crosses your face. Somehow, your bank account lights up, and you hear the musical sounds of money jingling... Ka-ching! That's the sound of this fifth personality characteristic.

This is not to say that Guerrilla Entrepreneurs are money-minded, for they are not. But it is to say that they know what it takes to obtain money. Not luck. Not a lottery. Not an inheritance, though we bad-mouth none of those. But aggressiveness. That's the trait we laud to the skies.

With every business utilizing just a handful of marketing weapons – 3, 5, 10, or even 15, the opportunity to choose from among 200 is a heady feeling. It takes an aggressive attitude to wrap your ambitions around such a lofty amount. But it's that aggressiveness that's going to separate you from the wannabe and wimpy guerrillas, if indeed, there is such a thing as a wimpy guerrilla.

We're not saying that you'll need all 200 weapons or even half of them, but you ought to be aggressive enough to want to know of their existence so you can select the ones that seem most appropriate for you. Successful Guerrilla Entrepreneurs have a large selection. You can find a list of them at our website at: www.gmarketing.com

When you learn that the average American business invested 4% of gross revenues in marketing in 2016, you're aggressive again. You think, "Only 4%? What if I invested 6%? 8%? 10%?" You know that the average business goes out of business within 5 years. The last kind of company you want as a benchmark is an average business.

You're aggressive in your thinking and in your investing. Guerrilla Entrepreneurs save money not by failing to spend it, but by not wasting it. Aggressiveness is your hallmark. You're among the first to use some of the new weapons of marketing. You probably have a blog. You've already begun podcasting. You've been hard at work compiling your opt-in list. This kind of aggressiveness is the sign of a leader.

Because you're aggressive in your thinking and your investing, your competitors fear you, respect you, follow you, and acknowledge your leadership. The media come to you for quotes, resulting in you getting the lion's share of free publicity. Very little goes to the lambs.

At a party or any social function, you may hide behind the foliage, speak in a soft voice, be a practicing wallflower. But when it comes to marketing, you're a lion. You're the king or queen of the entrepreneurs. You're a marketing titan – known for your visible and omnipresent marketing. As you may have heard, size doesn't matter. It's all about attitude. And yours is characterized by your aggressiveness.

The Sixth Trait: The Embracing of Change

You know it and we know it: the only thing certain is change. No matter what happens in the life of your business, change is the only certainty. How you deal with change makes an enormous difference in your success – or lack of it.

You can ignore change, hoping it will go away. But we're here to tell you that it won't go away. You can disdain change, detest change or fight change. Or, you can be a guerrilla and embrace change. Be careful in how you interpret this. Change for the sake of change is not a good thing. But change for the sake of improvement is a very good thing. Don't let your negative attitude or fear of change prevent you from benefiting from the improvements.

Face up to the fact that change will continue to happen all around you, especially in marketing. How you deal with that change is what makes you a guerrilla. Get to know change on an intimate basis. Love it or hate it, but don't pay it no heed. *Millions of people lost billions of dollars because they ignored Social Media.*

Millions more lost millions more dollars because they accepted it too soon and misused or abused it.

When we urge you to embrace change, we want you to do it at the right time and for the right reasons. That takes study. That means you must pay careful attention. That means not following the crowd but following your own good instincts. Don't make the all-too-common mistake of wanting to make a change but also wanting to wait for the prices to go down. While they're taking their own sweet time going down, you could be losing a fortune while competitors are building an insurmountable lead due to their willingness to invest at the outset while their own competitors are asleep at the wheel and saving pennies when dollars are at stake.

Embracing change is a matter of timing and knowledge, vision and guts. Guerrillas who possess this trait are rarely mired in the past and usually poised for the future. Does that describe you? We hope so.

The Seventh Trait: Generosity

Successful Guerrilla Entrepreneurs view their marketing as a chance to help their prospects and customers succeed at their goals. Whether that goal is earning more money, expanding a business, getting a job, losing weight, attracting a mate or improving their golf score, they try to find ways to help them achieve their goals. Knowing that we're living smack dab in the middle of The Information Age, they are very generous in providing information.

Sometimes that information is imparted by a website. Or it can be given in the form of an e-book, free report, consultation, seminar, or lecture. Often, instead of giving information, they give something of worth and value to their customers.

****

A series of apartment buildings in Los Angeles had a 70% occupancy rate. But one of the buildings had a 100% occupancy rate. How did this happen? That particular building put up a sign that said, "Sign a lease.... get free auto grooming." What the devil is auto grooming? That meant they hired a person to wash the tenants' cars once a week. The salary they paid the car washer was easily worth the difference between a 70% occupancy rate and a 100% occupancy rate. The building management simply asked themselves, "What might our tenants appreciate?" The answer was simple. And their generosity in regularly performing the simple act of a weekly car wash was the difference between a highly profitable building and a so-so profitable building. No rocket science here, only common sense and a spirit of generosity.

****

Ask yourself, what might my prospects and customers appreciate for free? A ballpoint pen? A calendar? A pocket calendar? A refrigerator magnet? The answer need not be lavish or expensive, but merely an expression of your generosity. Flowers, plants, free samples... these are some of the myriad ways you can prove your generosity. You'll see that they go a long way toward bonding with your prospects and customers. They're easy to come up with if you have the spirit of generosity, if that generosity is part of your personality. Bonus for you: it's fun to give rather than receive.

The Eighth Trait: High Energy

To practice constant acts of generosity, to consistently prove your imagination, to be aggressive in your deeds, to assess and accept change... all of those require a consistent display of energy. If you don't really have that energy, you can't really put your heart into all of your actions. And putting your heart to them is part of the deal. Customers know if you're doing something because you have to or doing that same thing because you want to. They're attracted to businesses that want to serve, that want to make their customers happy.

Because being a successful Guerrilla Entrepreneur is a full-time job that takes energy – not sometimes energy, but all-the-time energy. A ho-hum attitude is very apparent just as a willing attitude is easy to see. For that reason, we have seen that high-powered, highly successful guerrillas happen to be high-energy people. They bristle with energy. Everything about them is electrifying. They even spread their energy throughout their workplace, even away from it. It's no surprise that they get a lot done, moving forward at all times. They are quick to greet customers, sincere in their customer relations, ready to act without hesitation. They seem to want to take action. And the reason is that they are possessed of more than their share of energy.

That helps them to do the job at hand, then be ready to take on the next job. They are happy in their work, even awaken each morning looking forward to doing the work they love. That, by the way, *is a key to their high energy – doing the work they love. They know that by doing the work they love, they never work a day in their lives.* This love of work is always manifested by their high energy level. That's what it takes to do all the tasks at hand then be ready to take on more. You can sense their energy level when you see them work. Amazingly, they don't even work to demonstrate that energy. It is part of their overall personality. If you cannot make it part of yours, if high energy is not second nature to you, perhaps you should pursue a more mellow line of work. But if you can make it part of yours, you have the personality of a guerrilla who is bound for success.

The Ninth Trait: Constant Learning

Think of a seagull. It flies endless circles in the sky, endless circles in quest of food. When it finally spots the food, the seagull lands and eats its fill. Then it rises again to the sky, only to fly in endless circles again and again. Once more, it flies in quest of food. The seagull does this because this is its most powerful instinct.

Guerrilla Entrepreneurs have an instinct that is just as powerful, just as never ending. Do you know what it is? It is the instinct *for constant learning.* Guerrillas learn and learn and they learn some more. They are endlessly learning for *they've learned that knowledge equates with success.*

They realize that they are no longer in an age when they ought to learn all there is about a topic, but in an age when they ought to be learning one thing after another. As marketing changes lightning fast, Guerrilla Entrepreneurs do all in their power to continue learning about the new changes in marketing. At the same time, they are learning about the peripherals of marketing: psychology, the Internet, technology, Digital Marketing and the globalization of business.

Whatever they are learning, it is a constant endeavor, just as searching for food is a constant activity of seagulls. We have never seen an exception to this observation. Each guerrilla leader that we encounter seems to be engrossed in learning new things. Truly, that is a crucial trait in all of them. We hope and suspect that it is also a personality characteristic of you.

The Tenth Trait: Love of People

The people we have met who are running successful and profitable marketing programs know that all people are fascinating, all people are interesting, and all people – you may have to dig a bit to find this one – have a lovable side. "The softer side of Sears" is how that company termed it. The idea here is that all people have a softer side.

Guerrilla Entrepreneurs look for and discover that softer side, that fascinating side, that lovable side. This interest in people is apparent in their marketing, in their marketing people, in their treatment of clients. *Successful Guerrilla Entrepreneurs have learned that every person has a story.* By being superb listeners – a key characteristic of guerrillas – they learn those stories, *and adjust their marketing to fit the deeper and inner core of those stories,* and also, are able to adjust their own stories so that they are equally fascinating, equally lovable – or at least likeable.

Guerrilla Entrepreneurs know that every person is unique, each one is someone's son or daughter, father or mother, brother or sister. They honor this uniqueness by not treating every person alike. Their honest interest in people makes them masterful communicators. And that masterful communication makes the guerrillas themselves enjoyable to hear, to listen to, to learn from.

People who are not interested in other people are often not interesting themselves for they tend to talk about themselves. And that's rarely someone's main field of interest. Their prime field of interest is their own self. And they tend to listen to people who will talk about them, talk to them, care about them.

Show us a self-centered person and we'll show you someone who is not a true guerrilla marketer. Of course, everyone is not a guerrilla marketer. But all the people who run winning marketing programs certainly are.

The Eleventh Trait: The Ability to Maintain Focus

Many large and respected companies, with well-known names and abundant respect, figured that their business expertise would enable them to succeed in areas far from where they had been demonstrating their core competencies. Most of those companies, later having lost millions of dollars, realized that they were in over their heads because they allowed their corporate egos to ride herd over their common sense.

Guerrilla Entrepreneurs don't make that mistake. *They are skilled at their core competencies as well as being skilled at maintaining their focus. They do not worship at the shrine of diversification, but instead at the shrine of excellence.* Instead of going off into unchartered territories, they concentrate on adding even more excellence to their current endeavors. They strive to do what they've always been doing, only doing it better than they have before.

Technology and experience enable them to succeed at that goal. Those factors enable them to keep their focus while making it even more acute. Mind you, it's not easy to maintain your focus. In today's world, distractions abound. Side tracks woo many a leader from his or her chosen path. Almost always, trouble lurks at the end of those roads.

Maintaining your focus sounds easy but is hard. This does not mean that you should resist change but that you should accept it if it helps to keep you on track, on target, on the money. But if it causes you to veer from your target and diffuse your focus, steer clear of it. We have seen many train wrecks caused by following tracks that led off the edge of the cliff.

We have also seen many century-old companies earning more than ever because they were able to resist the temptation of novelty and corporate confusion while staying the course. Word of warning to start-up businesses: You will be tempted often to go for the gold at the expense of your focus. We have nothing to say against gold and only four golden words to say about focus: *maintain it or else.*

Trait Number Twelve: Taking action

In seminars, presentations, and assorted trainings we have done around the world, we have learned by simple before-and-after observation that people have one-way brains or two-way brains.

- People with one-way brains read books, attend seminars, take copious notes during presentations, pay rapt attention during trainings, study the Internet, learn from mentors, listen to CDs, watch DVDs, take courses, participate in tele-seminars, and learn as much as is humanly possible.

The information they absorb is assimilated, memorized, and understood. But it remains within them, which is no place for important information to reside.

- People with two-way brains absorb the same information, but then they take action on it. They know darned well that *GUERRILLA MARKETING IS NOT A SPECTATOR SPORT.* They realize that information not acted upon is wasted information. They act on the advice they are given. They breathe life into the concepts they have learned. They experiment. *They know that action is the name of the game to guerrillas.* Because they have two-way brains, they do something about what they have learned.

While others may learn by hearing, successful Guerrilla Entrepreneurs learn by doing. They are a very hands-on group of people. That laying on of the hands is one of their many secrets of success. If your personality does not include the proclivity to take action, change that aspect of your personality.

We are not writing this book as an academic exercise, but as a method for you to learn exactly what you must do to be a successful Guerrilla Entrepreneur. The key word in that sentence is "do."

PERSONALITY CHARACTERISTICS OF SUCCESSFUL GUERRILLA ENTREPRENEURS

1. Patience
2. Imagination
3. Sensitivity
4. Ego strength
5. Aggressiveness
6. Embraces change
7. Generosity
8. Energetic
9. Constant learning
10. People person
11. Maintains focus
12. Takes Action

[Note: For biographical details on the authors, please refer to p.30.]

CHAPTER 15

EXPOSE YOURSELF TO THE POWER OF YOUR NAUGHTY SIDE

BY CYNDI COON

I don't play by the rules. Call that naughty? I agree. Being naughty invites in creativity and unexpected magic. I grant myself permission to not only color outside the lines, I take the coloring book page, tear it up, write all over it and then craft it into something entirely new. This process is so liberating that others want to join in. So much so that I cultivated a tribe who not only embrace my behavior but encourage it. The transformational work I do explores how to channel naughtiness to expose creativity and use it as a super tool.

Why would clients want to work with a naughty rule breaker again and again? First let's look at what I mean by naughty? Acting naughty means being disobedient. Being disobedient means refusing to obey authority. My disinterest in going along with "the way it has always been done" means there was no other option than to strike out on my own. I held many jobs and I worked very hard at each one. I knew all along, however, that each job was just a means to an end. I listened and I learned but I never stayed for long.

I am rewarded with a practice that is now a series of projects that have a clear beginning, middle and end, and because there is always an end that means a change in leadership will always come. This is good for me because I push against authorities. A magical skill of mine is to be disobedient in a way that invites others to dig deep and call up their own courage to see what happens if they act naughty. I have clients that hire me again and again because they thrive when their ideas are pushed against. Many do not have enough people around to push them and say no to their first ideas. Our culture is filled with "Yes Men" and a whole population of "Just Tell Me What To Do" drones. I believe in asking the "what if" and "why not" questions.

My naughty tendencies will take a client's idea from middle of the road and push it to a point that will make them feel uncomfortable at first, but I will gift them with a magical "wow" factor and we'll meet in the middle at the end of it all. If their project is a boring academic conference with 400 in attendance I will take it, twist it up and turn it into a sideshow under a circus tent with 7,000 people. How do I do this? By filling every idea with a disobedient, non-conformist thought and asking far "outside-of-the-box" questions. These thoughts then grow into all new ideas, ideas that can't be born out of being well-behaved and questioning nothing.

What does it feel like to act naughty? It can feel nauseating. I consider myself a brave, bold soul, but each time I have to call up the naughty behavior in order to push a project forward, I have to dig deep to pull out my bravery. Just because I have the skills to call it up doesn't mean I am not scared every time I do it. The work is not in the doing but in the moments leading up to the doing. A perfect example of this is skydiving out of an airplane. The sailing in the air isn't the scary part. What is completely terrifying is the moment when the door of the plane opens and you fall forward out of the plane into the sky, that's it, everything else is smooth sailing from there. You have to be willing to open the door and fall.

I started to build tools long ago for summoning my brave self, but every time it still requires strength to take it on. My strongest tool for this job is confidence. Sometimes the confidence is right there, out in front, and then other times I have to "fake it till I make it." However, those times that I can only bring forth bravery by faking it, I always end up thrilled with the outcome. This is because no matter what I did that was naughty, I created something new into the world, even if only a simple thought or idea. It can feel scary to act naughty, but the whole world loses when people don't choose that course. I choose it everyday, scared or not.

I live by a motto of "let's try it!" I believe we should all step into a space where the rules don't have to apply and the object of the game is to continuously reinvent. This space is created by each of us giving ourselves permission to reinvent and permission to play differently. I am comfortable in confidently giving others and myself this permission. Not playing by the rules means asking, "What if there is more then one possible outcome?" or "Can there be more then one winner?"

I am a terrible consensus builder; it gives me a rash to even be asked to build consensus around an idea. I just keep thinking why do we have to decide on just one option? Why can't we take two or three possibilities, break them into pieces, rebuild them and come up with a totally different option number four? I say "Let's try it!"

Being a rule breaker can look like a lonely endeavor but the truth is, it is so rewarding to offer something unique in the world . . . that you give others permission to do the same. It's true that this will drive rule-followers crazy but that's what I'm here for – nothing moves forward without a push. They may join me or they may turn their backs and walk away, but in any case I always know that other like-minded spirits will show up. None of us are so unique that we can't find our rule-breaking tribe.

This act of breaking rules can feel agonizing to some. To not act like everyone else makes me feel vulnerable too every time I step into bravery. Here's the thing though, it can also feel freeing - I love this John Lennon quote about being a freak:

> *I'm not going to change the way I look or the way I feel to conform to anything. I've always been a freak...*
> ~ John Lennon

Growing up in rural Michigan incredibly poor, I was raised in a small community that focused on football, farming and little else, I was a freak and definitely did not fit in. Not fitting in was a good thing though, because it meant no one was looking at me to see that I wasn't playing by the rules. To be dismissed as an outlier is a gift. As a result of not fitting in with most people I created my own tribe. At times it was a tribe of only one other member but it eventually grew to many. If you don't have a tribe that gives you permission to be you - start building one. My tribe doesn't resemble the status quo and I definitely don't follow any rules on the company I keep.

One thing I will say about my tribe is if you act nasty then you are out. I welcome naughty but nasty means you are negative and that is never tolerated. I surround myself with only positive energy and people who support and like to spend time with other rule breakers. A party full of positive, focused, rule breakers will make a lot more happen in the world than a party full of rule followers who all color inside the lines. When the rule follower's show up, I have to remember they are there to build up my resistance.

My positivity kicks in and I recognize that I need to be strong enough to stand up to those who want to shut down ideas, opportunities and possibilities. This can feel lonely at times, but I have a magical skill of allowing time for pause, to slow down and to see what is happening around me. This is a skill of mine that works most of the time but sometimes I fail and I fully welcome possibilities of failure. By breaking the rules, I am failing more often then those playing it safe, but I learn more from that than I ever would if I followed the rules.

I am able to continue to do this because I have always surrounded myself by champions who support me. We support each other with a reminder that the world is better served when we stay true to ourselves. When we check our authenticity. It is important to have champions because they are honest with me even when I'm not ready for it. My champions will hold a mirror up and force me to look directly into it to ensure I am staying focused on what matters most to me. Being true to myself means embracing those things that make me who I am. Those things include listening to my intuition, having fun and practicing creativity all while taking risks. I am known for disregarding what is expected, I do this because I know that the minute I do the unexpected, something magical happens.

I have built my business and my brand around dedicating time to think. Time is the most valuable commodity to me. Therefore, I am not interested in investing my time in anything that remains stagnant, follows the rules, or conforms to what is expected. I spend my time both for my business and for my clients thinking about ideas that at first are so big they are hard to even verbalize, but in my gut I can feel there is a nugget of something magical present. I choose to listen to that small nugget of potential magic and allow for time to build it further.

Next comes the fun part, I love to co-create with my clients. In allowing for thoughtful time, together we design and create things into this world that are incredibly future thinking. It can be hard for companies and organizations to plan for much beyond the next two to three years. My role for them is to hold a space to look way far out into the future, say ten years to twenty years. This allows them to dream big without being focused on immediate outcomes, which can often block creativity and ideation. Holding this space for people means they have in me, a person to help form their ideas that often die without a champion. I love to serve as a champion of ideas for my clients, and it is why they hire me again and again.

At the end of it all, I want to lead a kick-ass life and that means coloring so far out of the lines that it's off the page and out of the book completely. If I am listening to myself, choosing the naughty path and making people nervous, then I am doing something right. Doing the unexpected, allowing magic to work, calling up intuition and demanding that projects are fun – takes guts. I operate much better when I listen to my gut. I have built a practice and a client list of people who love working with me because I give them permission to play, co-create and listen to their gut. My service in the world is to show up so big that everyone around me sees that as a possibility for him or herself too. People seek me out because they've heard I can help them imagine much bigger than they are able to do on their own, but people hire me again and again because they discover it is a fun time to be naughty and co-create magic.

About Cyndi

Cyndi Coon is a storyteller who sees the world in pictures. She connects with people to co-create big giant ideas as a thinker, experience producer and creativity advisor. She is a speaker, a writer, a teacher, a coach and a leader with contagious positivity and high energy! Cyndi is the Chief Experience Producer and Founder at Laboratory5 Inc.

Cyndi's clientele includes many companies and organizations in the S.T.E.M + A (science, technology, engineering and mathematics plus art) Industries. Often she turns the M in STEM upside down, changes it to a W and lists many woman-focused companies as her clients (S.T.E.W.) She also delights in working with academic organizations, leading the transformation path of science as performance.

Cyndi is an expert in stealing, inventing and shopping for time, intuitive ideation, and using creativity to expose clarity and experiential magic. Clients work with Cyndi to think into the future, to deepen their process and to leap to the next level with their teams, their ideas and projects. Her naughty, rule-breaking approach keeps everyone on their toes. Her vision of the world melds with her clients need to be pushed and think bigger in order to bring to life transformational outcomes. She has a distinct way of thinking that offers a unique perspective and pushes the boundaries to give clients pure magic. She has the industry nickname of *The Purveyor of WOW!*

Cyndi loves to explore, hike, camp, listen to music, read and create in her studio or on-the-go with her traveling creativity kit. She leads a fun life where she lives and works in a creative space located in the Sonoran desert.

Cyndi Coon received a Masters Degree in Fine Art from Arizona State University, Tempe, Arizona and a Bachelors of Fine Art Degree from Kendall College of Art and Design in Grand Rapids, Michigan. Cyndi taught at Arizona State University at the Herberger Institute for Design and the Arts. After years of teaching she has written the forthcoming book *Professional Presence For Creatives,* and co-written a book on professional creativity called *Creative Clarity.*

CONNECT WITH CYNDI:
- cyndicoon.com (Speaker / Author site)
- Laboratory5.com (Experience Producer site)
- Facebook: Laboratory5
- Instagram: lab5
- LinkedIn: cyndicoon
- Twitter: lab5

CHAPTER 16

RECIPE FOR SUCCESS

BY CHRISTINE SAMS

There is a recipe for everything we do in life.
~ Christine Sams

Perfection is the result of effort, not luck. In all the sales positions and careers I've ever held in my professional life, I was faced with a choice—which way would I execute a sale or a meeting? "Wing it" or "Prepare." *If your goal is to create something rewarding and sustainable there is only once choice—PREPARE.*

When we prepare a meal or bake a cake do we just go to the kitchen and start? No, we prepare in advance by making a list of ingredients and shopping for what we need. After that, we start our creation, using the time frame that the recipe shows. *Truly, there are recipes for everything we do in life.* **Baking that perfect recipe takes time, effort, and discipline!** I know from experience. Most of my adult life has been spent in sales, and I had a less than traditional approach at times, winging it and hoping for the best. Eventually, through trial and error and learning from the best in the business, W. Clement Stone and Napoleon Hill, I realized if my prepared presentation was in order, everything worked like a perfect recipe and – *tahdah* – SUCCESS would come. I'd found the *Recipe for Success.*

169

LIFE LESSONS AND TEACHING MOMENTS

Growing up in the Pacific NW near many ski mountains, I was fortunate to have my Aunt Alice, who gave me her skis when I was young so I could take advantage of those mountains. On Saturday mornings throughout the winter, my mum would get me up at 5 AM. Then she would drop me off to board the JC ski bus that would deliver me to Mt. Baker, eager and ready to delve into the ski mountain known for being steep and deep. As for me, I was under 5' and 12 years old and my skis were size 210. That's right! If you know skiing, you know these are heavy and long.

At first, my lessons were for the first half of each Saturday with friends. I was so scared. And did not have any control! The equipment was not perfect for me, but it was what I had. Continuing to try, I failed repeatedly. Eventually, I kind of got the hang of it—no broken bones! I realized this: **My instructor was good. It was me holding back my progress.**

Eventually, I returned to skiing as an adult—with new lessons and new equipment. It was just as challenging. Still holding back, but yes, I could ski. However, it still scared me and it was more work than fun.

One day, at Snow Bird, Utah, with deep powder and a steep mountain before me, I took a lesson, my fear still high. Avalanche Control had finished setting off dynamite around the ski slopes. I quickly found out this instructor was different. He understood that skiing was more than physical knowledge of how to execute. He watched my form and advised me that I was working so hard at skiing back up the hill that my body language was resisting the downward slope of the mountain. He coached me through my fears, making me the star of the story and helping me to adjust my thinking, my shoulders and skis to point down the hill. Hello gravity! *It began to ease me gracefully down the hill, changing my experience instantly.*

For years, I'd worked on physical form, but had poor results. One minor adjustment was all it took, along with an analogy that I related to. That day I went from a scared skier with little control to a graceful expert skier. Today, I conquer Triple Black Diamond Runs with no fear. It is one inspiration behind the Recipe for Success. There is no need to struggle; there is only a need to understand—and follow the recipe.

A popular phrase for sales trainers is: "Always be closing." This is true, but this is also true: **"Always be learning."** It seems like I'm always reading a book or taking classes in skiing, golf, sales, math, and Real Estate. Green is growing—always keep learning and growing as a person. If we stop, we die.

There are no secrets to success. It is the result of preparation, hard work and learning from failure.
~ Colin Powell

My father gave me this small book to use as a guide in living life. It is titled, *Rules for a Knight* by Ethan Hawke. I recommend you read it. In it you will find: *solitude, humility, gratitude, and pride.* This quote from Chapter IV (Pride) resonates with me: **"Never pretend you are not a knight or attempt to diminish yourself because you deem it will make others more comfortable. We show others the most respect by offering the best of ourselves."** Thanks, Dad! This is one of the best books I have read, and use this advice daily.

My mum also taught me many lessons. She always seems happy and content in the kitchen, baking and preparing meals. Watching her then and now when I am preparing meals or baking, is relaxing and calming for my soul. It inspires me, too! Precisely following a recipe leads to success. There is no "winging it." An extra ingredient (or leaving one out) is not a good idea. I say, "Be like Mum—follow the recipe and find success!"

I needed to become the master baker of my career and life!

171

TWO OBJECTIVES OF A GOOD RECIPE

It doesn't matter what we are selling, it's still the same recipe.

Regardless if you're selling wine, cars, insurance, or hospitals, the recipe is the same. A successful transaction feels good, complete, and comforting. When all the ingredients are in place everyone WINS! This is at the heart of what we are able to do in life.

When I began learning sales technique in the early 1980s, the message of consistency was a strong one. You didn't change proven recipes and techniques because times changed, because many aspects of human nature don't change! A good recipe endures time and lives on and typically it has an objective, or two, in this case!

Objective #1: Know your subject matter.
What do you plan on baking (selling)? Whether it is advertising, helicopters, software, homes, or buildings, you need to know your product and inventory. Learn it inside and out so you can provide answers to most questions. Don't make up information. If you don't know, let the client know that. Then find the answer as soon as you're able and convey it immediately. This shows your client that they are a top priority.

Objective #2: You need permission.
Permission is a very important part of your recipe. Otherwise you are baking without an oven—a guarantee that it won't turn out. Identify your audience and ask for permission.

For example, you sell insurance. Your audience is a small car lot. Start by asking for permission from the top of the company, whether it's the owner, president, vice-president, CEO, or general manager—go as high up as you can get! This is professional and courteous, plus it starts the conversation, giving you a chance to give your brief introduction.

Create your introduction, but don't gear it toward selling your product.
Use it to *introduce who you are* and to *ask permission!*

Permission resistant people are inevitable. You're communicating, you're excited, but they are not. How could they not be interested? Then it happens; you hear "No thank you." Those words stop many sales people dead in their tracks. They give up. Don't give up, simply understand and ask if it would be okay to talk to the employees about your product; if you could have a brief bit of time at a staff meeting or talk to employees during a lunch break. Offer up the option of talking during off-work hours. *Your diligence can make the difference!*

Whether you call on a company or a family or individuals, these two steps still apply!

Your two objectives can be met, regardless of the size of your audience when you take the right steps. Next…it's time to follow the recipe. Don't fall flat once you get an audience!

CREATING YOUR RECIPE FOR SUCCESS

All ingredients in a recipe are necessary! Don't skip out on one, because if you do, your recipe will fall flat. It's difficult, if not impossible, to add a forgotten ingredient.

Imagine this scenario…

You have permission and you are in front of the decision makers. It's your moment! It's time to start baking that perfect recipe. If you know the recipe and if you know how people respond, you'll be spot-on in your efforts. They'll have an appreciative smile on their face and an enthusiastic "please continue on" coming from their lips.

Start baking! Your recipe has ten ingredients, and they are all necessary.

- **Dress:** Always dress for success. This is respectful and important for your professional persona. You will look the part of an intelligent, successful professional.

- **The Introduction:** Shake their hands—not too firmly or too softly—and make eye contact while doing so. Remember names, using them in making your clients the "Star of their Story."

- **A Diversion:** Don't go right for the sale. Start with something that's off topic, even if it's weather or current events.

- **Camaraderie Building:** Create a common bond through finding a connection or common interest. Generate a sense of fellowship and community.

- **Determining the Need:** The people you are in front of have an inadequacy or insufficiency that your product can correct. Know what's missing. Explain how you can fill in the void.

- **Adding Value:** Highlight your product's value by knowing it inside and out. You'll want to state at least five important facts about this ingredient (but no more than eight). Paint a picture of the specific use they would realize by owning your product, making your clients the "Star of their Story."

- **Encouraging Questions:** Part of the "value ingredient" is not giving away so much that there are no questions. Questions build rapport and trust, while ensuring that your message and the benefits of your product are clear. Again, make your audience the "Star of their Story" with the information you've learned about them!

- **A Smooth Close:** There are as many closing techniques as recipes in this world. One that works well with the Recipe for Success is the "assumable close." If you follow the recipe you can assume your clients will move forward. They may even ask you what they do next to finish up. If they don't ask, simply say, "If you have no more questions, how would you like to pay?" Or, "Are you ready to move forward?" Then let them answer. Do not say another word until they do. Look at them directly in the eyes. They will answer, and it will likely be, "With a Credit Card."

- **Copies/Receipts:** Give your clients copies of contracts and receipts for the entire process. They should have this information! There is no better way to emphasize that you are their liaison.

- **Referrals:** Ask for referrals—always—because as long as you have correctly assembled your recipe, your clients will be happy to offer them.

DIRECTIONS FOR A SCRUMPTIOUS RECIPE FOR SUCCESS

Are you ready to follow the directions? Every recipe has them. Just embrace KISS (Keep it simple stupid) and you will be great. *This is a grass roots idea that works!* **A sale is a human interaction that assists in meeting a specific need. Don't overcomplicate it.** If you are focused, regardless of the size of the sale, you can utilize the recipe in the same manner. It's not about how high-tech or low-tech your product is. *The bottom line is that we are all people with feelings, concerns, friends, and families.*

By building stronger connections with individuals and decision makers, we often come face-to-face with them. This is where we rise to the occasion, connecting through:

- The inflection in our voice
- Our body language
- Information through words we choose to use

In preparing for that face-to-face meeting, we can do things to gap the amount of time it will take to make a connection that shows you care, and includes:

- Sound, professional communication via phone, email, or text
- Thoughtful research that shows you are entering into a situation with good information

Block out the technology when it comes to your meeting/presentation, even if your product is technology! Give your undivided attention, this is respectful. They are giving you their time and attention, reciprocate. Organic living resonates with more people every day, because it is authentic and there is no connection better than the human connection.

I told you—these directions are simple! Following them will lead to the perfect recipe, because you are handing every ingredient organically and with importance.

Believe in your product and yourself.
Don't sell, FACILITATE.
Be the problem solver or the joy giver.
You are the professional. Take the reins and administer each ingredient step-by-step.

PERFECT PRACTICE

■**Make a plan with your product or service.**
■**Develop a recipe using these guidelines and practice it repeatedly.**

You have the recipe and you know the directions. It's time to jump in and start baking! Mistakes will be made along the way. You're improving and you are aware. It's on you, not your manager. Embrace the process and evaluate it—always learn from it! The fears we don't face become our limits!

My recipe works and it will give you the confidence to eventually create your own recipe, whether it's based on what I've offered or an original based on your mastery of your sales craft. *And you'll know you're successful in the one way most people respond to:* YOUR PAYCHECK. In sales, the paycheck is the evidence that we are doing the right things. Money is not evil, it is a tool and a measure. That's what it is.

You know what I love most about this recipe? It also applies to life! Use it in your personal life as well. It's amazing! I've seen it. My associate and mentor, without even consciously thinking about it, applies the nature of this recipe to all his relationships, personal and professional. Because of this, he is respected by all that know him. *He's the type of person we want to meet. For most of us, he's the type of person we'd love to be.* And we can be!

Regardless of where you are in your sales career, I hope you can take away something from this chapter to help you grow. **Remember what you wish to achieve in your daily life and in business.** Do it with a smile, because a genuine smile can seal just about every deal! Not to mention it's a great way to brighten someone's day, including your own.

About Christine

As a Real Estate professional, **Christine Sams,** Broker, CBA, CIPS, Realtor has listed and sold more than 200 properties. Besides real estate, Christine has worked in financial planning, insurance and marketing throughout the past 30 years. She specializes in Residential Real Estate, Commercial and Investment properties, and Land for Development. Christine has assisted investors, builders, developers and buyers in property acquisitions to meet Real Estate and Financial goals. A number of local and national banks have worked with Christine to reduce their inventory. She has also assisted in acquiring and developing hospitals, senior care facilities and campus developments.

Currently Christine's focus is in assisting her clients in selling and buying Real Estate in the Snohomish County, Washington area.

Additional designations and memberships Christine is involved in:

- CIPS – Certified International Property Specialist representing clients both locally and internationally
- CRS – Certified Residential Specialist
- TRC – Transnational Referral Certification
- NAR – National Association of Realtors
- WR – Washington Realtors
- AMPI – Asociacion Mexicana de Professionals Inmobliarios (Mexico)
- Washington Realtors International Real Estate
- AREAA – Asian Real Estate Association of America
- SRES – Seniors Real Estate Specialist

She also enjoys traveling to Greece, Italy, Mexico, Asia and to her second home in Arizona. She enjoys horseback riding, snorkeling, skiing, golf, reading, collecting wine, photography, and writing.

Being a daughter, sister, mother, and friend have proven to be my best, most in-depth learning experiences in life and allow me to be the caring professional I am today.
~ Christine Sams

CHAPTER 17

SOLVING THE MYSTERY OF MARKETING

BY DEREK CHAMPAGNE

If something's too good to be true, it probably is. And if advice is too complicated to follow, you're probably not going to follow it. In contrast to a screed of complicated maxims, I'm here to impart to you two pieces of wisdom today. That's it! They are easy to understand, they are true, they are inextricably linked, and they can be scaled to your brand, your business, and your style. Think of them less as an unsustainable crash diet and more of the common sense, life-changing variety of simple truths: eat well, exercise when you can, and always wear sunscreen.

So, Dear Reader:
- **The first thing is that marketing doesn't have to be a mystery.**
- **The second is that marketing also doesn't have to cost a million bucks.**

Some of the best marketing—and certainly some of the most fun—comes from inventive folks in startups who are strapped for cash, from street teamers and guerrilla marketers, from people at gold standard companies who dare to think differently (namely, like they don't have a corporate line of credit backing them up if all else fails). And, I'm willing to bet, from people who are a lot like you.

I know this because I've been there. I've been passionate about marketing since an early age; I started playing in bands by the age of 10. Along with the love for the music came the need to take the mystery out of marketing. I remember creating my own branding, media kits, and websites; at age 18, when most of my peers were out getting into some good old-fashioned trouble, I applied for my first bulk mailing permit so that I could mail out hundreds of press kits each month. When I got some success under my belt (and the valuable perspective that comes with age), developing and selling two businesses before I turned 25, I went on to practice street team guerrilla strategies for bringing in an audience in a highly competitive music scene—Hollywood's Sunset Strip.

I'm at a point in my life now where I work with clients who have bigger budgets than I did when I was marketing my own music as a teenager, but that doesn't mean I've lost the lessons that I learned back then. Nor do I exclusively work on brands with big budgets behind them. But what brings all this work together under the same umbrella—no matter the brand, no matter the budget—is that I approach it all with equal parts innovation and discipline. And the thing about success built on strategy is that with a little elbow grease, it can almost always be replicated.

TEN STEPS TO TAKING THE MYSTERY OUT OF MARKETING
—And Making It Work On A Shoestring. . .

All I ever needed to know about marketing, I learned from a duck named Quackers. Well, that's not entirely true, but this one particular experience sticks out in my mind. So much so, in fact, that I recently published a best-selling book about my marketing philosophy, entitled, you guessed it, Don't Buy A Duck! Stop Wasting Money And Only Do Marketing That Works.

To briefly recap, I learned early on what it meant to blow your entire budget on a bad idea when, one lazy weekend afternoon at a yard sale, I decided that I simply must use not only my entire allowance, but also my brother's, on a handsome little duck (the aforementioned Quackers). I'd never had a duck before, had no idea how to take care of one, what I'd do with him, or what it would really be like to be responsible for this little living bird. Five minutes later, when we were driving down the road and Quackers was flapping around in the back of my parents' station wagon, I knew I had made a mistake. But, understandably, the yard sale had a strict no returns, no exchanges policy on live ducks.

Thanks to some neighbors, Quackers, no worse for wear, was able to live the rest of his life out in a peaceful pond. And for my part, what I learned was that just because you deep-down-in-your-bones want something doesn't mean it makes it a good investment. This is certainly true of marketing and brand building, particularly for today's professionals, who are often overtaxed and bombarded with choices and trendy toys.

I've dedicated my career to making sure that my clients avoid the expenditures and headaches that come from buying a duck, metaphorically speaking. And along the way, I've honed some tried and true tactics that address the common pain points of marketers—many of which can understandably eclipse one's better judgment when one gets intimidated by the "mystery" of marketing, the idea that it's a lot of guesswork and smoke and mirrors. When you systematically shine a light on the components of your marketing—your strategy, your needs, your tools, and so on—you don't have to worry about buying a duck.

1. **Solve your identity crisis: get a handle on who you are, who your clients are, who the competition is, and what you have to offer.** All too often, marketing feels mysterious when you don't have a clear idea of your identity as a brand. Shining a light on this identity means doing the (very fun, by the way) legwork of establishing clear reference points

for identity. In this case, I mean:
- a) The identity of your brand:
  - ◆ Who are you?
- b) The identity of your customers:
  - ◆ What market segment are you hoping to serve?
  - ◆ Who do you want to reach?
  - ◆ What are their habits, their specific needs?
- c) The identity of your competition and the landscape of your specific marketplace:
  - ◆ What needs are being left unmet?
  - ◆ Is there room for disruption, or for carving a particular niche?
- d) And the nuts and bolts of what you have to offer:
  - ◆ What sets you apart from your competition?
  - ◆ How do you want to be known to your customer?

Brainstorming the answers to these questions is a great start to really grasping your identity as a brand.

2. **Make your mark by staying on message.** Once you've worked out some of this identity stuff, there's a bit of reverse engineering to do to create your message. Let's say you're an insurance company, and you want your brand to embody an approachable, imminently trustworthy neighbor. What sort of messaging—everything from your logo and print materials to your social media presence—do you need to speak truth to this idea of your brand? Once you've crafted your message, make sure that all your marketing, branding and PR is in alignment with that message.

3. **Take an inventory of your toolbox.** We're living in a terrifically exciting time for guerrilla marketers in particular; the tools that are available to us via social media, Web 2.0, and analytics technologies (to name just a few things you should have in your armature) make it easier than ever before to make skilled marketing work on a shoestring budget. Think about your messaging and the identity you

want to impart to your customers, and where you want to reach them. What tools would best serve as means to that end?

4. **Build an integrated marketing plan.** If your marketing doesn't seem to be going according to plan, it could very well be because you don't have a plan. I'm a huge advocate of writing everything down—tools, messages, all that great information, and brainstorming on identity, demographic research, etc.—and building an integrated marketing plan that serves as a touchstone for everyone in your company from the C-suite to the cubicles. An integrated marketing plan gives you a reference point for everything your marketing and messaging needs to address. Think of it as a playbook that can help you get from one end of the field to the other.

5. **Set realistic goals.** When making your plan, be sure to include concrete, attainable goals to keep you going. The more specific you can get about your goal, the better. There's no cookie-cutter list of ideal goals, either; it's going to vary depending on your business. Some examples might be to aim for an increase in revenue broken down by time or demographic; to gain a certain number of new subscribers to your service; to penetrate a certain number of markets per quarter, and so on. You can further ensure these goals are reasonable by researching past performance, getting the lay of the land (and yes, the competition), and so on.

6. **Measure your progress.** Setting the goals is only half the battle. You want to make sure that you're making progress and that you're gaining momentum from this progress (and learning lessons from setbacks, rather than simply throwing good money after bad, or even worse, throwing up your hands and walking away). How do you eat an elephant, after all? One bite at a time. Looking at it another way, measuring your progress helps you break down the entire

football field into first downs for when you're making those plays from your playbook—it's much more manageable (and sustainable) that way.

7. **Build a better customer experience from the ground up.** Everything you do, especially if you're marketing on a shoestring, has to build a positive customer experience. You simply can't afford not to have your customer experience the promise of your value propositions; in today's world of instant information and social media, gaffes can be costly. What isn't costly are the myriad ways you can invest in a better customer experience from within your organization. How can you make use of the assets you already have to build a better customer experience? Do you have a customer service force that you can empower to make clients happy by any means necessary, like Zappos? Do you have channels that already exist, such as your website or blog, that can reach your loyal customer base and make them feel empowered, informed and attended to? These aren't things that take a lot of capital, but they certainly pay big dividends.

8. **Bring in brand ambassadors.** Your employees and your customers are your best assets; not just in the sense that they work for you (in the case of your employees) or they pay their bills (in the case of the customers), but in the sense that they are your boots on the ground. They are the people with the fantastic stories of the good works (and the goodwill) that your brand can generate. You can't put a price on the loyalty that comes with cultivating brand ambassadorship among your customers and your employees.

9. **Think outside the box with partnerships, PR, and promotions.** I mentioned at the start of this chapter that I got much of my experience with guerrilla marketing trying to stick out in a crowded marketplace as a musician. It was there that I learned the value of thinking outside the box— forging partnerships and connections other than the ones

that I was paying for. Once, my band mates and I forged a partnership with some of the top hostels in Los Angeles; in return for them advertising our shows, we would provide free rides to their customers. It was a smash-hit; eventually we ended up needing to outsource some of the work to other drivers when we ran out of girlfriends, groupies and friends to help pitch in. The hostels got unique customer service, we got audience members, and everyone was happy—and again, the gains far outweighed the costs.

10. If at first you don't succeed, adjust, adjust, adjust.
My last piece of advice is perhaps the most important. There isn't a cookie-cutter method for success. There is never going to be a formula that's going to get you amazing results every time—remember what we all know about things that seem too good to be true? It's inevitable that you're going to have to make adjustments to your plan along the way, and that's okay. If you learn from an experience, it's not a failure, it's a learning experience. I'd like to think that Quackers would agree with me. To that end, I've designed a system that's worked well for me over the years: PETMAG.

I could write a whole book on PETMAG – it's that helpful. A cyclical system for executing non-emotional marketing decisions, PETMAG (Plan, Execute, Track, Measure, Adjust, and Grow) is the wheel you need to keep moving forward. And adjustment is a vital part of that—it's how we get to GROW, after all.

About Derek

A true entrepreneur from an early age, Derek has always been interested in fostering connections and finding an audience, in both the marketing and music fields. The son of touring musicians, Derek quickly became comfortable engaging audiences and had formed his own band by age 10. He became obsessed with connecting services and products with the end user using the most effective message and marketing tools available. Derek developed and sold his first two businesses before the age of 25.

Now CEO of The Artist Evolution (www.theartistevolution.com), a marketing, design and campaign management firm he founded in 2007, Derek helps businesses of all budgets design and implement marketing strategies that work. He has developed and managed brands and marketing campaigns in multiple industries from start ups to household names. He has pioneered marketing strategies a variety of industries, and has used his twenty-plus years of advertising, branding, and marketing experience to build a formidable business.

Derek Champagne is also the best selling author of: *Don't Buy a Duck: Stop Wasting Money and Only Do Marketing That Works* (www.dontbuyaduck. com). Derek's formal education is a bachelor's degree in marketing and a Masters in Business Administration. He also attended Musicians Institute in Hollywood, CA where he focused on bass guitar and performance arts.

Derek also hosts a podcast, BusinessLeadershipSeries.com, that engages with leaders who are making an impact on their worlds, and want to share their knowledge and experience for the personal and professional growth of others.

Derek Champagne is endorsed by the ASDA as a trusted marketing resource, and he is an advisory board member and a guest contributor for the national publication, Dental Entrepreneur Magazine. He is a frequent guest lecturer at business conventions and college business marketing classes covering marketing and social media subject matter. Derek is also a nationally-published musician who has made musical contributions to the soundtracks of television shows on ABC, MTV, Bravo, Oxygen, and the E! Channel.

When he's not making music or marketing strategy, he enjoys volunteering for non-profit organizations in his home state of Arkansas, spending time with his wife and two children, playing his guitar, enjoying the occasional game of golf, and staying actively involved in his church.

For more information about Derek's agency, visit:
- www.theartistevolution.com

Or you can contact him directly at:
- Derek@derekchampagne.com or on LinkedIn

CHAPTER 18

THE TOP TEN ATTITUDES OF A SUCCESSFUL GUERRILLA ENTREPRENEUR

BY JAY CONRAD LEVINSON AND
JEANNIE LEVINSON

You go to a highly respected business school, earn an advanced degree in business, then find yourself out *in the real world* where, in most cases, *your attitude counts more than your education.* What do you, an up-and-coming guerrilla, do when reality clashes with book learning? You find out the attitudes of those guerrillas who are already living your dream, and then you adopt those attitudes for your business. Where do you learn the best attitudes for a guerrilla marketer? You learn them here and you remember that there are more than ten winning attitudes.

1. Passion:

Passion influences the other attitudes. It fuels your marketing fires, and energizes you beginning in your heart rather than your brain. Passion is different than enthusiasm because of the heat of the fires. It is different because of the level of the intensity. It's a matter of energy.

Extremely contagious, passion spreads from you to your co-workers, then to your customers, then to their friends. Your passion shows in every aspect of your business. Ideally, your passion is not something that you have to develop. If you're a true guerrilla, it burns within you with the light of its fires guiding you in the right direction and solving your problems.

****

"There are two great days in a person's life---
the day we were born and the day we discover why."
~ William Barclay

****

You already know about passion because it has motivated you to take marketing seriously and to be bright enough to start at the beginning rather than the middle, where most businesses start. One of your toughest jobs will be to find people who bring the same passion to the table. You might not be able to do that. But it doesn't bother you because you know you have enough passion for the entire company.

But do you? Will that passion generate energy even in a tough economy, even after business downturns, even after loss of a key customer or supplier? Will it be there eight years from now? If you've got the right stuff in the passion department, all the answers are yes. And eight years from now – oh boy! – you just light up at the ways you'll be able to exercise your passion then!

****

Take the Passion Test –
Go to: http://www.thepassiontest.com

****

2. Generosity

We investigated this attitude in detail back in Chapter Fourteen. We're not going to repeat ourselves, but we'd be remiss if we didn't include it in this list of top ten business attitudes. It's included because it's so rare.

****

We've spent the past few weeks furniture shopping, or more accurately, furniture buying. Visiting store after store, we've been treated to a broad array of good and bad attitudes. We realized that if the showroom is too generous -- "We'll give you those two decorator pillows, that rug and the ottoman if you buy today....and we'll toss in free delivery," – that made us wonder if everything we were buying was overpriced to begin with. "The floor model of this recliner sofa is the only model that's on sale right now. To get the fabric you want on that sofa would cost three times as much as this sale price." Although that was probably the truth, it didn't demonstrate the store's devotion to generosity, so we walked.

****

You've got to talk that fine line between too generous and not generous enough if you embrace the attitude generosity. *Embracing an attitude of overall generosity means that you not only practice generosity, but that it delights you to do so.*

3.   Speed:

Time is NOT money. You read it here first, unless you read it already in every other guerrilla marketing book since the 1990's. Instead, *time is life,* and your customers know it. If they sense that you're wasting their time and don't respect it enough, they'll find a competitor of yours that wouldn't dream of wasting their time.

Speed doesn't necessarily mean racing all over your office or store. But it does mean moving fast whenever there's the option of moving slowly. Let your customers see, hear, sense how oriented you are to speed. That will attract them as well as giving them some cogent words to say if they're engaging in word-of-mouth marketing.

****

"The electronics store we shop at has all their speakers in one demonstration room so we could sit on an easy chair and listen to many rather than walk and listen to just a few, saving both our time and our feet"

****

Recall that the cost of speed is zero. It's just a matter of attitude, and not just attitude on your part. When you hire and train people, be sure they understand the precious nature of time as well as you do and are just as willing to work fast in an effort to save the precious time of your precious customers.

Your business will operate at the speed of your slowest employee. Bottlenecks are toxic to companies dedicated to speed. If your customers have to wait in line anywhere – at your store, at a cash register, on the phone, online, don't be surprised if they become ex-customers.

Speed is not yet taken for granted, but pretty darned soon it will be. Until that day, your attitude of speed and never wanting a customer to wait, will give you a competitive advantage. Keep your eyes open for businesses that adopt a time-based strategy. You'll be seeing more and more of them as more and more customers come to realize that time is life.

4. Sincere Caring:

We'll bet you know the difference between caring and sincere caring. Customers expect caring. They do not expect sincere caring. Customers aren't necessarily made to feel good by caring. They feel very good when they experience sincere caring. Caring doesn't show. Sincere caring is very obvious.

If you adopt an attitude of sincere caring, it will shorten the time before you have a multitude of warm relationships. As with the other attitudes in this top ten, sincere caring helps your company the most if everyone who has customer contact displays it. If just you display it, that's nice, but that's not overwhelmingly nice.

Businesses that demonstrate caring are the kind that might or might not be there for you in a pinch or when you have trouble with your purchase. Businesses that demonstrate sincere caring will always be there for you in times of strife and will happily go to bat for you with top management or a recalcitrant supplier.

They actually go out of their way to prove that they care. You can tell them by the way they ask questions and look you right in the eyes, by the way they attentively listen to your answers and have an intelligent response to them.

****

How does an attitude of sincere caring come about?
Two ways:
• Brilliant Hiring
• Brilliant Training

****

If you accomplish the first, it will be that much easier to accomplish the second because you have role models and potential trainers. One of the most winning aspects of all of these attitudes is the cost. There is none.

Still another winning aspect is the profit potential of these attitudes. There is plenty. Mark our words.

5. Honest Friendliness:

I'm guessing that you know what we mean by "honest friendliness." There's a world of difference between it and phony friendliness. Almost everyone has a radar that indicates whether the person talking to them really means what he says or is just going through the motions.

Listen, it's tough to deal with prospects and customers hour after hour, day after day. Most salespeople wear down in the process, but they can't leave the office and they want to keep their jobs, so they loosen into a state of false friendliness. Notice their lack of eye contact, absence of enthusiasm, lackadaisical body language, half-hearted smile. They definitely know the words, but you just can't hear the music.

When you have a staff of trained guerrillas who are able to practice honest friendliness whenever they're on the job, your prospects and customers can hear the music. They can have a meaningful dialogue with your sales people. They trust them. They buy from them. How much did this cost? You know it cost nothing but exceptional care on your part during the hiring process, and non-stop conscientiousness when it came to training.

In a perfect world, whatever that is, your people wouldn't have to be trained and you wouldn't have to be so cautious when hiring. But as we said earlier, many sales people get tired and suffer from energy meltdown at times during the day. To combat that reality, hiring and training will be keys to your success. Yes, there are honestly friendly people out there, people who are just plain fascinated with other people. Cherish these people. Hire them and reward them well. But don't expect them to be easy to find. You should be on the constant lookout for bright and shiny people. But we think that what the others don't have at birth, they can get from you.

It's obvious that there's a world of similarities between sincere caring and honest friendliness. Both are rare. And that's precisely why companies that are blessed to have them on staff are rare themselves and provide an atmosphere that makes customers feel comfortable in your surroundings and confident in your business.

More and more, it's becoming recognized that *one of the secrets to success in business is to create a pleasant buying environment.* That doesn't necessarily mean a dazzling showroom. It also means people who make prospects and customers feel good throughout the entire experience.

Who are those people? You knew the answer before we even wrote it here: people who exhibit sincere caring and honest friendliness.

****

Years ago, the Bahaman Islands were experiencing a slump in tourism. It seemed that natives resented the tourists, the tourists sensed it, and started choosing other places to take their vacations.

To combat this, the Bahamian government started teaching their young children in school how important tourism was to their economy, and that is what enabled their parents to be able to afford to buy them things.

They taught the children to make an effort to be friendly to the tourists, helping them feel welcome, by greeting everyone they met, making direct eye contact, and giving them a big smile.

After some time, tourism made a comeback in the Bahamas, and if you travel there, you will notice the friendliness, especially among the children and now young adults.

Their government learned the business value of sincere friendliness.

****

6. Neatness:

Two of the most successful business operations in the history of earth are Disneyland and McDonald's. Everyone who has visited any Disneyland is impressed by the cleanliness, the neatness, the absence of any mess. One of Disney's policies is to be sure the restrooms are cleaned every fifteen minutes.

****

Once, we spent a chunk of time at Epcot in Disney World in Orlando. We decided to sit down and spend some of that time observing people litter. Sure enough, the visitors littered with the best of them, but the litter didn't remain on the ground more than five minutes.

It seemed that Disney employees appeared from behind shrubbery or dropped from clouds to make the litter disappear. Disney knows that neatness is an all-day endeavor.

****

What are the things that people like most about McDonald's? Number one is clean restrooms. Number two is good French fries. You'd think that their success had something to do with hamburgers and prices. But you'd only be half right. Clean restrooms are number one on the list. And the fries are pretty darned good.

What's the main reason that women select the service stations they do? Answer: clean restrooms. Nothing about octane or prices. Everything about neatness.

When people see that your premises are neat, they assume that you run the rest of your business that way. When people see the premises are sloppy, they figure that's how they'll be treated in a pinch. You'd be appalled if you knew how many people never make a purchase in a place that hints of dirt – anywhere.

Interesting fact: one of the world's biggest neat freaks was Ray Kroc, founder of McDonald's. Another world class neat freak was Walt Disney. It's notable to realize that their inherent neatness was one of the reasons for their outstanding success.

You won't hear the word "neatness" in most marketing lectures, even at the best universities. But you will read it in the marketing plans of McDonald's, Disney, Nordstrom and a host of others. It is our hope that you become one of those others, because neatness is an attitude that equates very closely with profitability.

7. Telephone Demeanor:

Of all the minority groups on earth, the most special to you are the people who call your business on the telephone.

Are your customers made to feel like interruptions of your business or like the reason you're in business the first place?

All too often, potential customers call a business, are treated discourteously by a busy operator, then cross you off their list as a source of what they want to buy.

Anyone who answers your phone just has to be trained in the proper way to treat callers. Those *callers should hear a smile in the voice of the operator, should sense a desire to please, should be made to feel important.*

****

Once, we were called into Midas Muffler Shops because they were dismayed at their inability to make appointments with callers. Midas was getting 100% of their initial contacts by the phone, which is wonderful, but they were converting only 71% of those callers into appointments, which is terrible. It meant they were dropping the ball 29% of the time.

While surveying the shops in person, we couldn't help but notice that most of the time, the ringing telephone was answered by a person who obviously didn't want to be on the phone. That person was too busy, in a conversation with a customer, in a bad mood, or an introvert. Whatever the reason, the person answering the phone didn't want to be doing that – and it showed. No wonder so many callers failed to make an appointment for a new muffler.

We suggested a telephone training program to Midas. It would take only half a day. Midas was so warm to the idea that they instituted a new rule: "You can't answer the phone at a Midas Muffler Shop unless you've taken this telephone training." Within six months, Midas began converting 94% of all callers into finished appointments. That represents over a million dollars in profits, yet the cost was negligible.

We pointed out to the Midas people the importance of outstanding customer service and explained that customer service begins with the phone. We emphasized the need for warmth and friendliness, for patience and the ability to never seem to be in a hurry. We told them that bad moods are illegal on the phone and that introverts are not encouraged to answer the phone. Simple guidelines. Easy-to-listen-to advice. Common sense. It was presented so clearly that only one training session was needed. This was not information that had to be pounded into someone's head. It was straightforward advice that was easy to remember and easy to implement.

****

We can't emphasize strongly enough that you can institute, then implement the same kind of telephone training. You can transform all your callers into friends, and many of them into customers. Do it right at the start of running your business. It's the guerrilla way.

The same warm attitude should be apparent on your electronic telephone answering equipment: friendly message, caring attitude and helpful information.

8. Value:

Is value really an attitude? Or is it only an attribute that propels business? Of course, it's both. Just because you happen to offer a sleek new automobile rated highest by the most respected automotive reviewers yet priced at $3,000 lower than your closest competition -- does that mean your value, along with your quality, service and selection are enough to take your prospects over the top and onto your customer list? Barely. So give yourself a boost by exuding quality in your décor, attire, interior furniture, and restrooms. *There are you, selling $75,000 cars, and here are we reminding you to clean the toilets.*

It is that exquisite attention to detail that can make you confident enough in to radiate confidence in your marketing. That's a value attitude -- it showcases the real value that's up ahead. To communicate it, act like a winner. Assume that everyone shares your attitude and knows how good you are. That assumption will make value part of your perception.

If value does, indeed, become part of your very essence, good things will begin to happen. You'll discover *that it's easier to sell on value than on price.* You'll see that *the price-shoppers aren't as loose or mellow as the value shoppers.* Which group do you suppose would best qualify for an enlarged price transaction?

People who purchase for considerations of value are seeking reputation, brand awareness, safety, all the usual niceties, plus a fair price. Fair is a low price plus the person's perception of your value. Their perception will rise in accordance with how lavish you are with your details – related to your product or service, or related to you or your company. You'd be amazed if you knew the things that are perceived as value.

Not surprisingly, high price is amongst the leaders.

****

We were involved with a national hair conditioner product with sagging sales. It was packaged in a very handsome and beautifully shaped bottle, but the contents were pretty much the same as all the other conditioners in the category. We tripled the price. Sales more than tripled. People figured that if it's so expensive, it must be good.

We do not advise that strategy except to clue you in that raising prices is not the worst thing in the world.

****

No product category in America is led by the lowest-priced brand. We just want you to realize that if you sell solely on price, other price-cutters will constantly woo your price-conscious customers away. If you sell on value, you have a much better chance of maintaining a profitable long-term relationship.

9. Easy to Do Business with:

You've often heard it said – at least we have – *that it's easier to deal with failure than success.* We've seen that be true many times. Overexpansion, naïve hiring, poor financial management, overpromising, silly time management, unreasonable egos – those are a sampling of the perils of success.

The perils of failure are more fixable.

****

A remarkably successful and young company had doubled its sales each year since it started in 1972.

At a Board of Directors meeting in 1991, the Chairman announced that 1992 would be devoted to no growth. The gasp from the directors was clearly audible.

He explained that the company was no longer able to say "yes" to every customer request, no longer able to provide next day service, and in short, had become difficult to do business with.

"We'll be devoted in 1992 to saying 'yes' to all requests, providing next day service 365 days a year," announced the president. "We'll become easy to do business with once again."

*Perhaps it's because the company became so customer compliant that the following year, they were purchased by a **Fortune 500** company for a staggering sum of money.*

****

If you can winnow out a lesson in this tale about the value of superlative customer service, your company will gain from it.

If you haven't, we feel compelled, since this is the dawn of your guerrilla marketing ventures with your business, to remind you of something that becomes more of what you should be about each time you're exposed to the thought.

First, think this thought: YOU. Your business is not about that person. That person helps make things smooth and pleasant for the truly important people, your prospects and your customers. Those are the one who count. They're the ones you must empathize with at every opportunity. There is no way on earth that you can't arrange to say "yes" to their requests. They want next day service? You find a way for them to get it – and for the other people like them to get it.

I tremble when I call a bank. I know I will be treated courteously by a machine then put on hold, and sometimes permahold. There's a good chance I'll be transferred at least once and an off chance I'll be dropped from the line and forced to begin the process again. Many banks, especially mine, are not very easy to do business with.

Your mission is to be very easy to do business with. People might not do a dance of joy when they're about to call you, but they don't tremble either. And more calls equal more profits.

10. Flexibility:

What might be an effort for you is now a given, an act of kindness taken for granted by your customers. They know their parents didn't have it like this, but hey, it's a competitive world, and you've got to *offer flexibility or perish. Inflexible things become brittle and break,* while flexible things have long life spans and attract customers who will patronize your business for a long time -- or at least as long as you consistently demonstrate your flexibility.

It's crucial to know about flexibility as the outset of your guerrilla marketing attack. By starting with it, you won't be knocked off your chair the first time you're asked to prove yours. Although you won't be asked to put your flexibility on display many times a year, you must have it ready to rumble at all times.

Flexibility has more to do with service and product than it does with price. It has more to do with timing that it does with money. You can probably survive whether or not you have price flexibility, but you'll gain priceless word of mouth if you have service or product flexibility. Whenever I've experienced it, I told literally hundreds of people – simply to show them that small companies aren't the only ones that strut their flexibility stuff.

****

A woman was seated on a plane next to Phil Knight, the chief of everything at Nike. The woman mentioned that she had MS and always had trouble finding properly designed shoes. Phil Knight, living by his "Just Do It" mantra, took a meticulous measurement of the woman's foot and lower leg, along with her mailing address.

Three months later, a package arrived at the woman's door. It was a pair of one-of-a-kind Nike shoes designed for one individual with MS.

****

THE TOP TEN ATTITUDES
OF A SUCCESSFUL GUERRILLA ENTREPRENEUR:

1. Passion
2. Generosity
3. Speed
4. Sincere Caring
5. Honest Friendliness
6. Neatness
7. Telephone Demeanor
8. Value
9. Easy to do business with
10. Flexibility

[Note: For biographical details on the authors, please refer to p.30.]

CHAPTER 19

THE TOP TEN ATTRIBUTES OF A SUCCESSFUL GUERRILLA ENTREPRENEUR

BY JAY CONRAD LEVINSON AND
JEANNIE LEVINSON

We hope you're not misled by our top ten choices. If we had more time, we could have made a case for 200 choices. Our fear is that you'll become so focused on these ten that you won't aim your gray matter at other attributes. So say after us, "I (state your name) promise to open my mind to more than merely the top ten attributes, and will consider them a path more than a final destination. That crucial point I acknowledge and swear."

1. Name:

While beginning your march forward into your first guerrilla marketing venture, be extra careful not to stumble with your first step. Many companies do, which is why so many have misguided and misleading names.

To prevent yours from faltering at the outset, there are be-sures to help you do a bang-up job.

- Be sure it breaks the rules. Names that easily fit in with the crowd are names that are easily forgotten. Your name should command attention right at the start, then maintain that attention throughout the life of your business. If it reminds you of any of your competitors' names, drop it before you help them.

- Be sure it forces your competitors to wince. Your registered brand name is something they can't take away from you, so be sure it makes them feel uncomfortable. It if makes them squirm and they can't copy it, you've done a good job in the naming department.

- Be sure it is simple to pronounce and spell. Hah! We should talk with a name like "guerrilla." 80% of people who visit our website spell it wrong, forcing us to buy up all the misspellings and to name our website www.gmarketing.com. Hey, do as we say, but don't always do as we do. Especially in the easy-to-spell department.

- Be sure it tells a story or makes a promise. Truly good names are like teeny-tiny poems, like "Lean Crusine." Each letter, each word, each sound should work with the others to deliver a message. The right name will actually attract customers to your business. That's only one of the reasons why it is such a potent marketing tool.

- Be sure it suggests a feature or a benefit. Think of the most powerful benefit that you offer, then create a name around it. When customers see your name, they will be clear about what you offer to them. How many names fail to do that? Most of them. Don't let your name be one of them.

- Be sure you take a chance with your name. Putting it into the comfort zone is like putting it into the invisible zone. Make people sit up and take notice the moment they see or hear your name. If they read it, then forget it, you didn't take a chance. Guts and courage are part of the name game.

- Be sure you don't name yourself into a corner. Don't call yourself Pied Piper Children's Furniture if there's a chance you might become a purveyor of general furniture as well. Don't be Blake and Austin's Repair Shop if Blake and Austin might not be partners for life. Don't let your name prohibit you from expanding, diversifying or growing. Name changes are like having teeth pulled, only more painful.

The keys to bad names are those that are tough to pronounce, limit your business, exaggerate, or might remind folks of another company, and those that are spelled "guerrilla" because they're a bear, not a gorilla, to spell. You know our feelings about those.

If you're going to use the yellow pages, remember that names appearing first on a list get the majority of calls. So start your name with an A or better still, AA or even better, AAA. If you have a short name, you can use larger letters in your ad. A large name looks more impressive in marketing than a small name.

Your name can work for you or against you or just sit there and not work at all. As you get only one chance to make a first impression, you also get only one chance to name your company at the outset. Want to venture a wild guess as to which part of your business gets the most use by the most people? You got it – your name.

2. Branding:

Fish gotta swim, birds gotta fly, guerrillas gotta brand or they'll be lost in the fray. It's your branding that's going to help people trust you. That's what's going to break down the barrier between never-heard-of-you and can't-wait-till-I-talk-with-you.

Branding reassures people that they aren't the first lemmings off the cliff.

****

We were driving to an ad agency presentation and spoke excitedly about the presentation we were about to make. The cab driver turned his head to say, "You guys really believe that advertising stuff works?" He was definitely not an ideal customer. Or was he? "It doesn't work for me," he added. "I never would buy a product because of advertising. Never have. Never will." One of our people asked him, "What kind of toothpaste do you use?" "Oh, I use Gleam," he said, "But it has nothing to do with the advertising. It's because I drive a cab and I can't brush after every meal." Such is the power of branding. To him. To you. To me.

****

Your product or service can be more than a product or service. It can be a brand-name product or a brand-name service. That means people will have faith in you more than others and will even pay more money to purchase what you've got for sale.

Some brands are so embraced by people that they sport tattoos attesting to their loyalty. Harley-Davidson is a case in point. And we use the word point intentionally, feeling only a tinge of guilt.

It should be apparent that you probably can't brand yourself overnight. Like most great marketing, it takes time. And commitment. And consistency. *Without consistency, there can be no brand. It's the repetitive exposure that ingrains a brand in people's unconscious minds,* ready to spring into action when they're in a buying situation.

Branding seems to favor the visual depiction, such as Tony

The Tiger or Golden Arches, but it also seems to favor the verbal form, such as Coca-Cola or Mmmm…Mmmm…. Good. The idea is to have any kind of a repeatable, simple, understandable, venerable brand.

If you want to go for the gold, realize that the gold follows the people who have earned brand name awareness. Get it in the print media, the electronic media, the Internet, word-of-mouse, billboards, wherever you can. But get it as soon as you can. Waiting is the opposite of branding.

3. Positioning:

Why does your business exist? The answer to that question is your position. The closer that position fills the needs of others, the more primed for success you are. Every single business has a target market. What, specifically, is yours? A target market is made up of unique individuals. Conceptualize just one of them to get insights into what makes them tick. Are there a lot of people like the one you just visualized? If there are, you've got a strong position.

You've also got competition, or you will have it very soon. What is it about your position that will woo their customers onto your customer list?

All you've got to be is three things:
- Unique
- Desirable
- Believable

Be those three things and you've got the foundation of a powerful position, a powerful brand. So what is the difference between a position and a brand? Positioning relates to people and how they perceive you. Branding relates to your product or service and how they perceive it. A position is the essence of your product or service; a brand better be the same or you ought to send it packing.

What a position does is create a brand for you, a path to follow, a willing population of customers. It's much easier to create a brand if you have a clear position. You can't be all things to all people so what thing or things will you be? And to whom? Those people are wanting to get to know you. They know an appealing brand when they see it. And they know a position that fills their needs.

Your ability to position yourself exactly as enough people hope will determine your profits, your brand and your success.

4. Quality:

Last century, quality was a marketing strategy. Companies decided that they would provide the utmost in quality, and thereby capture a healthy share of market. It worked. Ask Rolls-Royce, Rolex, Ritz-Carlton.

That was last century. This century, if you don't have quality, the nice folks show you to the door. *Quality is the price of admission to being in business these days.* And if you haven't got it, guerrilla marketing will speed the demise of your company by exposing your shabbiness to more people faster than ever.

In order to do that, you've got to know what quality is, and most people don't. They think it's something they put into a product or service. Guerrillas know that *quality is not something that you put in to your product or service, but something that your customers get out of it.* Think they give a fig for how many grommets you used in making your gibbet machine? They do not. All they care about is what they get out of your gibbet machine? They are so awed by performance that they're oblivious to where it came from.

That's why most tests of quality have to include the human factor. Yes, the steel must be strong, but it must also be soft and silky and gorgeous and alluring at the same time. Quality is not what it used to be. The more characteristics of quality that you can measure, the more quality you can demonstrate to your customers. So get off of your wavelength and on to theirs to get the true meaning of quality. Seeing it through their eyes is not as important as feeling it in their hearts.

One of the most adorable aspects of quality is its ability to affect price. By offering more perceived value, the visual side of quality, you are able to sell at higher prices – meaning higher profits and more competitors. When there more competitors, the one with the most quality wins the blue ribbon.

5. Location:

It used to be that the business with the best location in town was the one at the high traffic location with the outrageously high rent. Now the business with the best location in town is the one at the no traffic location with no rent because it's just a spare bedroom with a computer that grants you online access.

You no longer need a lavish environment to earn lavish profits. But you do need a hard-working, intimately understood computer. And it helps immensely if you've got a good start on compiling a mailing list you can call your own.

World headquarters is as frequently a kitchen in a rural house as it is a skyscraper in Bombay. It used to be that you needed an expensive office location to be an international company. Now all you need is an email address anywhere where you can connect to the Net.

Do you have to be walking distance from your best

customers? Driving distance? Flying distance? Nope. Now all you've got to be is clicking distance. You can do business from your home in LA with another firm in Kuala Lumpur, also operating from a private home. Proximity to customers becomes virtually irrelevant in a world where every location becomes the best location, and anyone who can type has the potential to be an international entrepreneur.

Of all the sparkling advancements for business spawned by a new century, winning the space race and going the distance are two of the most beneficial.

6. Opportunities to Upgrade:

A customer decides to make a $1500 purchase from you. He's with you – in person, on the phone or online – and you let him know that with a second $1500 purchase, he can get free delivery. He ponders a moment then takes you up on your offer because two $1500 purchases are probably fragile, not to mention heavy.

Bingo! You've upgraded the sale and it didn't cost you a dime. Ever hear of free marketing? You just have. Who better to sell an upgrade or related product or service to than a satisfied, positively thinking, obviously present customer?

****

Upgrades come in a wide variety of forms:

- *delivery*
- *installation*
- *service contracts*
- *extra parts*
- *companion pieces*
- *deluxe versions*
- *complete packages*

****

The thing to keep in mind is that the people to whom you're selling really and truly want you to suggest a way for them to improve their lives by enlarging their purchase size from you. You'll let them do that and you'll toss in a discount at the same time? How good is that?

While earning their admiration, you're also earning ours, because you to deftly put into action this potent way to pump up your profits.

It used to be that when people got upgrades, they felt very special because of the exclusiveness. People still feel special, but they expect an upgrade all along. Do it and do it as much as you can. During an economic downturn, savvy businesses manage to give their profits an upturn by enlarging the size of as many transactions as they can. At the same time, many of them raise their prices substantially. To justify this tactic, they say "during an ugly economy, it doesn't make sense to try and buy the cheapest. Instead, you don't want to make a purchase mistake – and this price helps to assure you of the quality and durability you should be seeking."

7. Referral Program:

Your greatest source of new customers is old customers. They know you, trust you, have done business with you, and already have a relationship with you. Add to that insight the realization that every customer you have is the center of a network – with an impressive array of people to whom he or she can refer to you: business associates, neighbors, friends, relatives, fellow club-members, even acquaintances.

Be sure you tap this omnipotent referral power of your customers. To get them to refer you, simply ask for referrals. It's that simple and that straightforward.

****

One of the nation's most successful insurance salesmen was interviewed on a radio show. When asked when he begins to get referrals, he answered, "The moment I've made the sale."

He pointed out that the customer is then in a positive mood, wants to share your benefits with others, and is all too willing to help you out. The insurance salesman said, "As soon as the customer signs on my dotted line, I reach into my pocket take take out a small notebook in which I've written the numbers, one, two, three, four and five. Then I ask him for the names of five people who might benefit from hearing from me. Because I'm only asking for five names – and email addresses when possible, the simplicity of my request combines with the positivity of the moment and I'm usually given five names."

****

Two or three times a year, you should send brief emails to all of your customers, asking the same question, requesting only five names. You'll be very pleased at how many good names you get, and the cost to have such a referral program is the usual investment – time, energy, imagination and information – but not money.

Train your employees to ask everyone for referrals, explaining that by getting referrals, you're able to keep your costs down. The phone operator at the dentist's office who asks, "Is this appointment for you or for members of your family as well?" understands the simplicity of getting referrals.

If you want to add extra potency to your quest for referrals, ask customers if you can use their names – or best of all, if you can write letters for them to sign in your effort to secure referrals. Always keep in mind that when you seek referrals, you are really doing favors for people. You're in business because you believe you're good at what you do. Spreading the word about your prowess is hardly a sin. It's something that guerrillas do as second nature. Be sure you don't brag. Be sure you're totally honest. And be sure you don't hold back on this free way that guerrilla marketers earn their stripes.

****

The MMS Phenomenon:
Stands for the "Moment of Maximum Satisfaction." This is from the moment the customers makes a purchase and lasts for up until 30 days following after that date. This is the period that you will get the most referrals from your customer.

****

8. Credibility:

The path to profitability is paved with credibility. Guerrillas do everything in their power to earn this credibility. And there is a lot that they can do. Their website gives them credibility. So does any advertising that they do. PR stories give it do them, and so do articles they publish, talks they give, interviews they grant.

Because trust is the leading factor why people patronize a business, smart business owners knock themselves out earning this trust because they know it equates with credibility. If you have no credibility, it's going to be very difficult for you to grow, to earn profits, to make sales. People have to believe in you before they'll believe in your products or services.

During the start-up phase of a business, guerrillas make a list of the gucrrilla marketing weapons that give them credibility. Then, they set out to employ these weapons in their efforts to make this credibility part of their brand.

In fact, branding is a form of credibility. So is reputation. So are testimonials. As credibility itself is priceless, so are the manners of gaining credibility. You don't have to spend a lot to get a lot of credibility. Everything good that you have done in the past is another component of your credibility. People love to hear of your past actions because it reassures them that you're no fly-by-night operation, that you're for real, and that other people also see you that way.

Contrary to what you may have heard, people do not like to be pioneers. They want to know that others have benefited from doing business with you. Instead of being the first member of the community to do business with you, they want to be the 100th.

****

Can brand new businesses earn instant credibility? A few days ago, we went into a computer store because we needed some specialized service on our computers. The man we spoke to reassured us that his company could do just what we needed. When we asked how long the company had been in business, we were told, "This is our first day." The service technician must have seen the look of concern on our face. So he added, "But between the five of us who work here, we have a total of 55 years in business." Credibility takes a long time to build – but there are examples of instant credibility. That's just one of them.

****

9. Testimonials:

It's pretty hard to have a galaxy of testimonials the moment you launch your business. So begin to get them the first day you begin operations. When anyone says anything good to you about the way you run your business, ask if they'd consider putting their words into writing. Be honest enough to tell them how much this means to your business because you're brand new.

Testimonials are economical, believable, and versatile. I know one woman who papers a wall of her reception room with testimonials. Some of them are ten years old. That's still another advantage of testimonials: long shelf life.

****

When compiling your list of testimonials, realize that those signed by "T. Smith, Texas" aren't nearly as impressive as those signed by "Julie Townsend, Vice-President, Bank of America."

****

You can use your testimonials in a variety of ways: as a page on your website, as part of your sales presentation, as a page in your flipchart, as part of your proposals, as headlines for your ads and brochures. Here's a hint: the more testimonials you have, the better. Some people, concerned with "white space" in their marketing materials, keep the number of testimonials down to three or four. But profit-minded guerrillas have learned that the more testimonials they include, the more people will be impressed. This is no time for modesty. If ever there was a time to blow your own horn, it's the time you unleash your testimonials to a public that wants to read them, that wants to learn more about you, that cares what others think about you, that yearn for credibility in the company they're about to patronize.

Considering their power and ability to motivate others, it's almost too easy to get testimonials. Asking for them is hardly asking for the world. And having them can really mean the world to your business.

10. Reputation:

All you've got to do to attract business simply because of

your sterling reputation is handle the the hundreds of details of running a business every single day in every kind of situation, and do it for at least five years running. It can happen in three years, but before that, your time will be spent laying the foundation for that reputation.

The foundation will include your overcall consistency, your level of service, your ability to handle displeased customers, your way of using the telephone, your neatness, the attitudes of your personnel, and, as if I had to spell this out for you, the quality that customers receive from your offerings. In many companies, value is also part of the equation.

Probably, the most important of these factors in earning a reputation is the first one we mentioned – the consistency you display. One slip-up and you've seriously sabotaged your reputation for such a long time that you'll wince when you learn it.

****

We happened to be in Paris the year that front page newspaper coverage was given to the news of a famous restaurant being demoted from four stars to three in the respected Michelin Guide.
The restaurant critic explained that he ordered a dish in white sauce and thought the sauce was inappropriately seasoned. Zap! One star gone. You can be sure it will take up to a decade to earn it back The critic elaborated, "When you have the highest possible rating that we bestow, you are not allowed even one chink in the armor."

****

And that's the way it goes with reputations. In under a week, a TV spot can evolve from concept to finished commercial earning profits for your business. For a reputation to begin earning those profits takes a whole lot longer, but you must trust us on this one: it's worth the wait.

Of the many methods of marketing that money can't buy is your reputation. You don't buy it. You earn it. As powerful as a reputation may be, never forget that it's also fragile. It's far easier to hire a bad representative of your company than a good one. But a bad representative will cost you far more than a good one will earn for you. Remember the delicate nature of your reputation when you hire anyone.

****

THE TOP TEN ATTRIBUTES
OF A MARKETING GUERRILLA

1. *Name*
2. *Branding*
3. *Positioning*
4. *Quality*
5. *Location*
6. *Opportunities to Upgrade*
7. *Referral Program*
8. *Credibility*
9. *Testimonials*
10. *Reputation*

[Note: For biographical details on the authors, please refer to p.30.]

CHAPTER 20

TWELVE DIFFERENCES BETWEEN GUERRILLA WANNABE'S AND SUCCESSFUL GUERRILLA ENTREPRENEURS

BY JAY CONRAD LEVINSON AND
JEANNIE LEVINSON

1 - Wanna-be's obsess about ideas.
  **Guerrilla Entrepreneurs obsess about implementation.

2 - Wanna-be's want more web traffic.
  **Guerrilla Entrepreneurs focus on sales conversion.

3 - Wanna-be's focus on positive thinking.
  **Guerrilla Entrepreneurs plan for multiple contingencies.

4 - Wanna-be's want to get on TV and get "famous."
  **Guerrilla Entrepreneurs build their list.

5 - Wanna-be's seek a perfect plan.
  **Guerrilla Entrepreneurs execute and adjust the plan later.

6 - Wanna-be's wait for their lucky break.
Guerrilla Entrepreneurs engineer four, five, six plans and execute them in tandem, wagering that at least one plan will get traction.

7 - Wanna-be's fear looking stupid in front of their friends.
Guerrilla Entrepreneurs willingly risk making fools of themselves, knowing that long-term success is a good trade for short-term loss of dignity.

8 - Wanna-be's shield their precious ideas from harsh reality, postponing the verdict of success or failure until 'someday.'
Guerrilla Entrepreneurs expose their ideas to cold reality as soon as reasonably possible.

9 - Wanna-be's put off practicing basketball until they've got Air Jordan's.
Guerrilla Entrepreneurs practice barefoot behind the garage.

10 - Wanna-be's believe what they're told, believe their own assumptions.
Guerrilla Entrepreneurs do original research and determine what paths have been already trod.

11 - Wanna-be's believe they can do anything.
Guerrilla Entrepreneurs do what they're gifted for and delegate the rest.

12 - Wanna-be's think about the world in terms of COULD and SHOULD.
Guerrilla Entrepreneurs think in terms of IS and CAN BE.

[Note: For biographical details on the authors, please refer to p.30.]